THE GREAT BARRIER REEF

THE GREAT BARRIER REEF

WRITTEN AND PHOTOGRAPHED BY ALLAN POWER

SUMMIT BOOKS

Published by Paul Hamlyn Pty Limited
Sydney·Auckland·London·New York

Summit Books
Published by Paul Hamlyn Pty Limited
176 South Creek Road, Dee Why West, NSW, 2099
First published 1969
2nd Impression 1972
3rd Impression 1974
4th Impression (limp) 1977
© Copyright Paul Hamlyn Pty Limited 1969
Produced in Australia by the Publisher
Typeset in Australia
Printed in Hong Kong

National Library of Australia Cataloguing-in-Publication Data

Power, Allan.
  The Great Barrier Reef

  Index.
  First Published, Sydney: Hamlyn, 1969.
  ISBN 0 7271 0118 8.

  1. Great Barrier Reef. I. Title.

919.43

CONTENTS

TO DELPHINE

AUTHOR'S NOTE

Due to the fact that some species inhabit holes
or the underside of coral boulders,
several echinoderms illustrated in this book
have been placed to enable a clear illustration of the
particular specimen.

The illustrations of the animals so recorded are marked *

ACKNOWLEDGEMENTS

My grateful thanks go to the following for their
encouragement, advice and assistance.

Keith Gillett
Alex and Col Murtagh
Elizabeth Pope
John Yaldwyn and the Staff of the Australian Museum

Designed by Barbara Chapman

INTRODUCTION

Australia's Great Barrier Reef is one of the natural wonders of the world and along its 1,200 miles or more the underwater life is immensely diverse and beautiful. The animals of this area are not only subject to increasing research by scientists but they also incite the interest and imagination of students and the general public.

This book provides a fascinating glimpse into this extraordinary world and it is beautifully illustrated with underwater photographs in natural colour. Allan Power, the author, has been diving for 21 years, since he was 14 years old. The fact that he has won several national and international competitions in underwater photography is not surprising when one examines the magnificent plates in this volume.

Allan Power has provided some interesting and original observations and he has taken us, by means of his photographs, into the world of the skin diver - a world becoming more and more popular but still not experienced by the majority of people.

His observations highlight one of the most complex and challenging branches of science—animal behaviour. It has been said that anyone with patience, a sharp eye and ear, and a careful scepticism about jumping to conclusions can profitably study animals and may make observations of value to science.

Allan Power has shown himself to be such a person and he has also enforced the idea that a study of behaviour patterns of different animal species expresses their relationship just as well as a study of their body forms. In a way he was forced into this study since it was necessary to observe some animals for long periods in order to obtain the best photographs. It is a pity that more people do not use the camera for study instead of souveniring animals.

Even though this book is not written for the scientist he will find much of interest and value in it; the man in the street will be fascinated by the diversity, habits and behaviour of some of the most beautiful and spectacular animals in this underwater environment. Even those fortunate enough to have visited the Great Barrier Reef will be introduced to groups of animals rarely seen or recognised as such and they will have the additional pleasure of possessing some of the best underwater photographs ever taken, photographs of animals in their natural habitat.

John S. Lake,
Senior Lecturer in Biology,
The University of Sydney

CORALS

CORALS

Whatever one may read about the wonders of the marine life in tropical seas, one's first experience of swimming underwater over a coral reef is like discovering a completely new and exciting world. The tiny fish with their jewel-like brilliance, and the fascinating shapes and colours of the other creatures, all give one the impression of visiting for a brief moment a delicate and intriguing, secret and silent domain. It is a delight to watch the fish swimming about freely in their natural environment, unafraid as yet of human intruders. All one needs to enter this strange marine world is a glass-fronted mask, a pair of flippers and a little confidence.

Delicate, colourful, fascinating, exquisite; all these adjectives describe coral. Dangerous, razor-sharp, brittle, poisonous; this too is coral. Coral growths can be seen and admired but not all can be treated with impunity. When swimming underwater in and around reef areas, the only way for a diver to avoid coral cuts is to be clad from head to foot in a wet suit or some other protective covering. To the sailing-ship mariners of the past the dread of encountering a mass of coral reefs must have made life a nightmare. Even today, with the help of modern electronic equipment, vessels may still become trapped in a bewildering field of coral banks, with ultimate escape posing a major problem. So rapidly do coral reefs grow in some regions that charts become all but useless within twenty years.

Evidence of past shipwrecks is to be found along Australia's Great Barrier Reef but there are usually few identifiable remains to be seen. An odd length of corroded anchor chain may be discernible, or the shape of some massed coral beds may suggest that their foundation was part of a wrecked ship. There was little or no chance of surviving an early shipwreck in such a region. A vessel was soon pounded to pieces by the incessant battering of heavy seas. Survivors were washed against and across the growing reef, driven by the surf and horribly lacerated by the razor-sharp coral growths. Coral can cut through wet skin so efficiently that an injury will often pass temporarily unnoticed. If left untreated the wound can become infected, leaving an ugly scar when it finally heals. The creature responsible for the origin of the corals, and for the injuries they cause, is known as a polyp. Commonly of tiny size, it was once classified as a plant by scientists of the sixteenth century, and later as an insect. When Ferrante Imperato suggested that the coral polyp was in fact an animal, he met with the ridicule suffered by so many who have been years ahead of their time. Two centuries were to pass before his discovery was accepted.

Close examination of a bleached specimen of branching coral will reveal many small cup-shaped depressions or pores known as corallites. Within each corallite are a number of upright partitions called septa. It is the presence of these well-marked limy walls that helps to distinguish the true stony reef-building corals. In the living state each of the corallites houses a coral polyp. Thus a piece of branching coral is not the creation of a single animal but is the result of the combined efforts of a group or colony. The often delicate flesh of such coral polyps is not only surrounded by limy skeletons but is also internally supported. The colours of nearly all living reef-building corals are contained in their flesh. The agents largely responsible for these usually attractive hues are microscopic plant cells called algae, which occur throughout the tissues. These plant cells are so small that a single coral larva one millimetre long has been estimated to contain a total of 7,400 cells. Although the relationship between these plant cells and living corals is not yet fully understood, it has been proved that one of the functions of the algae is to assist in the formation of the corals' limy skeletons. It is thought that they probably also act as an automatic means of excretion, removing for their own use the waste products of the flesh of the corals. This type of mutually beneficial partnership between organisms of different kinds which live permanently attached to one another is known as a symbiotic relationship.

The mouth of a coral polyp is surrounded by tentacles, each of which is provided with numerous minute stinging capsules containing barbed threads immersed in a toxic fluid. On contact with tiny floating creatures, invisible to the naked eye, these threads are shot out with speed enough to penetrate and paralyse the prey. The victims are then usually passed by the tentacles to the mouth of the polyp. They are rapidly digested in the simple stomach cavity, and subsequent waste is discarded through the same single opening by which the food originally entered. Generally little food is captured during the hours of daylight, for then the tentacles of most reef-building coral polyps are retracted. With the coming of darkness the microscopic food organisms rise in far greater abundance towards the surface of the water, where the polyps' tentacles, which are then expanded, can more easily ensnare them. A few species of polyp do not manipulate captured food by means of the tentacles, but convey it to their mouth by the vigorous beating of tiny hairs or cilia. Living corals are sedentary growths which must rely on a sufficiency of drifting prey; water movement is very important for the supply of both food and oxygen.

Corals reproduce sexually by means of ova and sperms, and asexually by a dividing or budding process which can produce quite large colonial growths from an initial polyp. During breeding a polyp may develop either ova or sperms, the latter being released into the surrounding water as a milky fluid. Ova are retained within a polyp's body cavity, where they become fertilised by sperms taken in through the mouth opening. The resultant larvae, or planulae, then escape to enjoy a short free existence. The rhythmic beating of their surface hairs enables them to swim and float slowly near the surface. Finally they settle somewhere, become attached, and develop the characteristics of a tiny polyp complete with a supporting limy skeleton.

The so-called stony or calcareous corals occur in every sea, penetrating even to the colder northern and southern regions of the world. True reef-building species, however, cannot thrive in water temperatures of much below 68°F. Water temperature is also important in determining the variety and abundance of species, the branching forms of coral thriving best in temperatures of 74°F and upwards. The larger amount of calcium carbonate present in warmer seas provides the necessary ingredient for reef-building corals which reach their greatest development in tropical parts. A specially important factor is the limit in depth at which the reef-builders can thrive. Below thirty fathoms the intensity of light is not strong enough to maintain the minute plant cells living in the tissues of their flesh. When these symbiotic algae are absent the corals cannot thrive. In normal conditions, the more favourable the temperature of the water, the greater is the growth rate, but this is thought to be arrested when the coral reaches a certain size.

The great bulk or foundation of coral reefs consists of cemented limestone—debris accumulated over centuries and composed of compacted dead coral skeletons, coralline algae, mollusc shells and the powdered remains of myriads of other lime-secreting plants and animals. On top of this mountainous marine graveyard is the comparatively thin layer of living growths we think of as the reef.

The nearer corals are to the seaward edge of a reef, the better they grow and thrive, but although the waves there bring both food and oxygen in greater abundance, they also bring devastation. Stormy seas are the greatest factor in the destruction of reefs, with cyclones doing by far the worst damage. The heavy pounding of the waves tears the branching corals to pieces, and even heavy dome-shaped brain corals are often dislodged. Subjected to years of weathering, these become the great jagged boulders which stand like sentinels on the exposed reef.

A much less spectacular but very important cause of coral reef destruction is heavy, tropical rainfall. This can cause coastal rivers to pour enormous quantities of silted fresh water into the sea for many miles offshore. The consequent lowering of the salinity level and the smothering effect of the silt can convert large areas of growing reef into limestone desert. It is significant that breaks or openings in fringing coral reefs are generally found to occur opposite the mouths of the rivers. The resistance of some growths to the minor settlement of sediments varies greatly, depending largely on their capacity to remove it. Some do this by vigorous and sustained beating of the minute hairs or cilia on their surfaces. There are about 340 different species of corals on Australia's Great Barrier Reef, but some are difficult to classify because of the many and varied growth forms which occur within each species. Such differences depend upon the location of a growth. In a sheltered spot it may take on a branching form, yet in an exposed position be only a stunted, barely recognisable example of its species. Of the many types of corals to be found on a reef the fragile branching species such as the staghorn corals, and the denser, solid and rounded brain corals are the most common. A feature of staghorn corals, *Acropora*, is the usual antler-like form of their branches. In some cases, however, the growths tend more to resemble the branches of a tree or part of a tangled hedgerow. They are to be seen in abundance at low tide over reef flats, either as isolated colonies or in crowded array in deeper pools. As with most other forms of reef life, these corals reach their greatest size and perfection of form in the deep water beyond a reef's edge. Here some of them occur as great coral beds hundreds of yards long and up to four feet in height.

In the lagoon at Lady Musgrave Islet cay on the Great Barrier Reef are some of the largest and most delicate staghorn growths I have ever seen. Also there is a particularly crowded and rich, colourful array of various other corals little affected by wave action and free from the adverse effects of exposure. One must, of course, swim underwater in order to appreciate fully these magnificent coral gardens. However, even in the large surface pools, luxuriant growths of a common staghorn encircle the limestone margins. Here the coral growths consist of expansive horizontal plates with numerous stunted vertical 'shoots'. Anyone stepping on to such apparently solid platforms could be abruptly plummeted into the water, and could suffer serious lacerations.

The colours of these staghorn corals are particularly varied and beautiful, ranging through blue, heliotrope, purple and lavender to greens and browns. Some of the staghorns are the most spectacular of all the coral species.

The general name of brain corals is commonly used for a number of the solid and dense growths that are usually dome-like in form. These are found widely distributed over the whole area of a reef. The name derives not only from their shape, but from the convoluted brain-like pattern of the more typical of them. Particularly large hemispherical species to be found on a reef flat measure as much as twenty-four inches in diameter. In deep water beyond the reef's edge are other huge and dense boulder-like growths, *Porites*, which are fine in surface texture, have irregular outlines, and can measure up to twelve feet across. Hollowed-out caverns around their bases provide refuge for a great variety of the larger reef fishes.

While wandering over a reef flat, discovering the many varieties of stony coral growths, one is likely to see some soft slimy masses with a texture resembling that of a mushroom. These belong to the subclass Alcyonaria and are closely related to the true stony reef-building corals. While all are polyp-bearers, their surface pores or corallites lack the upright limy partitions present in the true reef-builders. Two outstanding types have hard calcareous skeletons which are characterised by their permanent colouring. One is the organ-pipe coral, *Tubipora*, with a bright red skeleton and greenish polyps that expand during the daytime. The skeleton consists of upright, elongated tubes reinforced at intervals by thin horizontal platforms. The other calcareous type, *Heliopora*, is known as blue coral and is, by comparison, far denser in composition. It does not expand its polyps during day-light, and when broken, it reveals the colour from which its name is derived.

The so-called soft corals are in striking contrast to all other alyconarians. They may take the form of crowded growths of delicate, naked polyps, or masses of a tougher semi-rigid nature distributed profusely over the reef flats. The only calcareous material present in these soft corals is in the form of extremely small, needle-like spicules scattered throughout the flesh. Colours range from a delicate shade of blue to greens, greys, bronze and drab brown shades.

Most beautiful of all alcyonarians are those named gorgonians or sea fans. Their massed growths assume the most fantastic of shapes, in many cases appearing more like plant than animal life. They inhabit deep water beyond the edges of coral reefs. Their usual colours are particularly brilliant reds and yellows. These corals often reach a height and breadth of three feet. Favoured habitats are overhanging ledges and coral-lined caverns or grottoes, which can only be reached by the skindiver. It is fortunate that these beautiful corals are never found uncovered by the tide. Even from their position below the surface of the water, they are far too often torn away and brought to the surface by the unthinking, who find that they quickly dry out, become brittle and finally crumble away.

Below: Fragile Staghorn Coral, *Acropora*, grows in shrub-like clumps and provides shelter for numerous varieties of small fish, North-West Island, Capricorn Group

Above: Staghorn Coral growing in deep water in a sheltered lagoon. Long, delicate branches like this would never survive in rough water. Fitzroy Lagoon, Capricorn Group, thirty feet

Right: Expanded, flower-like Polyps of Dendrophyllia wait to ensnare any food that comes their way. Living in shade under coral ledges in deep water, they lie contracted for most of the day, but begin expanding in the late afternoon. Heron Island, Capricorn Group, ninety feet

Above: Close-up of Dendrophyllia Polyps showing tentacles surrounding the centrally situated mouth

Right: *Mopsella*, a type of alcyonarian, showing the expanded feeding Polyps with their characteristic single circle of eight feathery tentacles

16

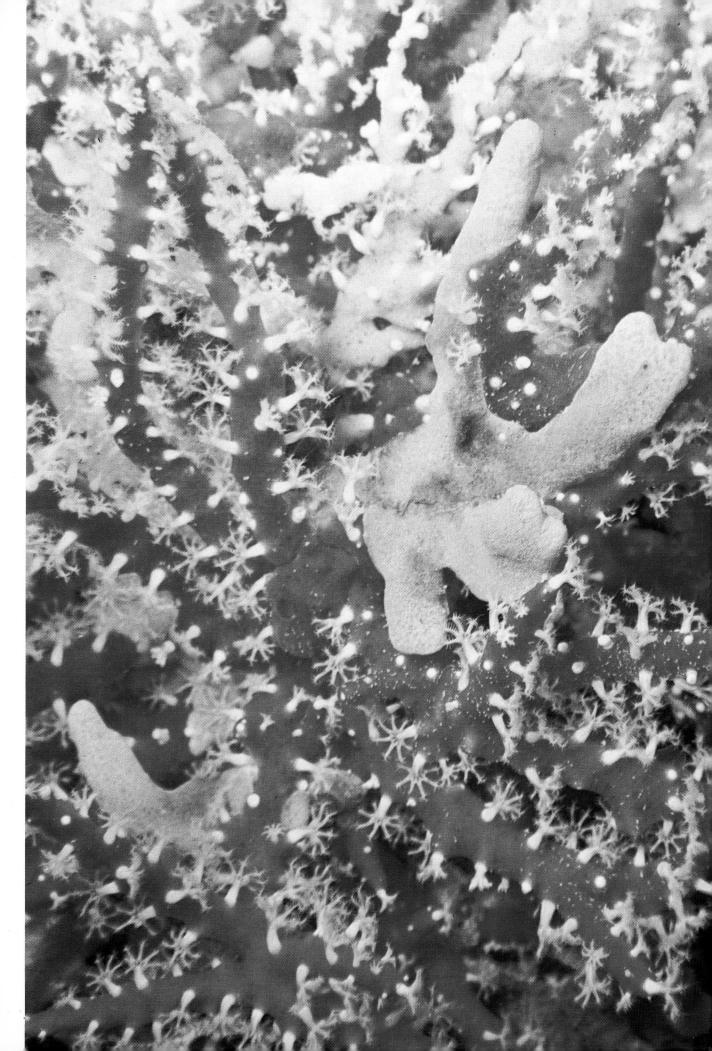

Above: A group of alcyonarians, the upper finger-like branched growths are a flexible, but horny Gorgonian Coral. Lower lobe-like growths are the soft coral *Sarcophyton*

Left: Demoiselles swimming among a garden of soft and stony corals. Tabular growths are another example of Staghorn Coral, *Acropora sp.* The red fan-like growth is a Gorgonian Coral, *Mopsella ellisi.* Wistari Reef, forty feet

Right: A Pink Parrot Fish feeding on Brain Coral. Mainly herbivorous, they remove vegetable matter and invertebrates from the coral with their strong parrot-like beaks. As coral is also removed with each bite, Parrot Fish are an important source of coral reef erosion

Above: Brain Coral, *Platygyra lamellina*, as it appears in day-light with the Polyps retracted

Right: Brain Coral, *Lobophyllia*, with the typical deep, convoluted brain-like pattern from which the general term Brain Coral is derived

Left: A Gorgonian or Sea Fan, **Mopsella ellisi**, growing on an old anchor ninety feet deep off Wistari Reef. This plant-like alcyonarian has a flexible skeletal core of a horny material called gorgonin. The Polyps, which are very sensitive to strong light, are usually only expanded at night

Above: Large tabular growths of Staghorn Coral, **Acropora sp.**, often provide safety and shelter for fish like this pretty five-inch long Butterfly Fish, **Chaetodon rainfordi**

FISH

FISH

The use of an aqualung allows one ample time to study and photograph the activities of fish, for settling in one spot without moving is a much better method of fish-watching than when free swimming. Areas which at first appear deserted, pulsate with life if a diver is patient. The fish soon accept the intruder, and fearlessly allow themselves to be photographed. Occasionally one sees the speedsters of the oceans, the magnificent mackerels, trevallies and giant tunas, but such sightings are simply a matter of chance, because these large carnivorous fish are wanderers who inhabit the open sea.

This is not so with the majority of coral reef fish and a diver operating in the same area for several days soon begins to recognise the true inhabitants of the reef. Each fish has its own little retreat or territory which it defends against any intruder large or small who blunders into its private domain. I have often stayed motionless in the one spot, much to the dismay of some tiny coral fish, and it can be amusing to watch the fishes' behaviour as they try to scare so large an intruder from their particular territory. Becoming highly agitated they dart to and fro until eventually a sharp nip on arm or leg serves as a none too gentle reminder to move on. As all the residents of the nooks and crannies among the corals guard their holdings so jealously, untenanted places affording shelter and safety tend to become scarce, so the fish soon colonise man-made debris on the sea bed. A wreck, lying on an otherwise bare area, bearded with weed and covered by shellfish, soon attracts and becomes the home of numerous varieties of fish. The great attraction is the labyrinth of tunnels, for fish love to have several safety exits. Once installed, fish will remain in their chosen habitat for some years.

By far the most common of the multitude of fish to be seen on a coral reef are the small, laterally compressed members of the family Chaetodontidae which, with few exceptions, are the most beautiful fish inhabiting the tropical seas. Appropriately called butterfly fish, they seem to flit above the corals like butterflies in a garden and their range of shape and pattern is fantastic. They are quick and active in their movements, darting to and fro with sudden stops and turns. They do not appear to frequent caves but prefer instead to live among and above the coral branches, where they rely on their alertness to escape from their enemies.

There are probably more than fifty species, all of which characteristically have small mouths with many small teeth. The family name, Chaetodontidae, means bristle-tooth. The small mouth, which in some species is set at the end of an extremely long snout, is ideally suited to pick tiny invertebrates, among which are crabs and other crustaceans, from cracks and crevices in the coral. The beaked butterfly fish, *Chelmon rostratus*, which grows to five inches in length, is an excellent example. Many chaetodontids have a unique type of protective coloration in the form of a large dark ocellus or eye-like spot, located on the rear of the dorsal fin. The real eye usually has a vertical band running through it, thus effectively camouflaging that part of the fish's body most difficult to conceal. The purpose of these unusual markings is believed to be to deceive predatory fish, for a foe striking at what appears to be the eye meets empty water as the quarry darts away. Chaetodontids inhabit all tropical reefs and a large variety of these fascinating fish is to be seen along Australia's Great Barrier Reef. One member of the family which is known to live only in Queensland waters is the pretty Rainford's butterfly fish, *Chaetodon rainfordi*, which grows to five inches in length.

Species of the genus *Heniochus*, the members of which also belong to this same large family, have greatly compressed bodies and bony projections or horns above the eyes. One of them *Heniochus acuminatus* has the fourth dorsal spine greatly elongated into a pennant-like filament which is usually at least as long as the body. Some individuals have extremely long pennants, but eventually these become tattered, and break or are bitten off by other fish.

Distinctive for their beauty and colour in a world of beautiful fish, the angel fish of the sub-family Pomacanthinae are considered by many people to be the most ornate of all the chaetodontids. Even their movements are majestic and stately. Individuals will often leave the protection of the coral boulders among which they live, to inspect a diver. They have a habit of swimming towards one and then, with an arc-like turn, presenting the full beauty of their weird and intricately patterned bodies. Some angel fish attain a length of two feet, while the butterfly fish usually grow no longer than six or eight inches.

Angel fish, although otherwise resembling the butterfly fish, may be readily distinguished by the strong spine on the lower margin of the gill cover. Also young butterfly fish usually have a pattern similar to that of the adults, so in many cases the juveniles are not difficult to recognise. However, among the angel fish, juveniles and adults are often vastly dissimilar. For instance, the juvenile stage of the imperial angel, *Pomacanthus imperator*, is dark blue with curved white lines on the body. The adult has about twenty fine, yellowish bands extending obliquely along the purplish body, and a dark saddle over the eyes which gives it the appearance of being masked. Needless to say, these differences between juveniles and adults have led to great confusion in the classification of angel fish. On occasion, the same species at different stages and with different patterns has been given different names.

Angel fish abound among the coral reefs of most tropical seas. They rarely take a baited hook, so they are sometimes speared by fishermen who relish them as food. The angel fish most commonly encountered around the southern islands of the Great Barrier Reef is the zebra angel fish, *Pomacanthus semicirculatus*, a striking species edged with electric blue.

The wrasses of the large family Labridae are colourful fish inhabiting shallow waters of coral reefs; there are over sixty genera, made up of about 450 species. Some grow to quite a large size, feeding on shellfish, crabs and seaweeds. They may be distinguished from the parrot fish they so closely resemble by their individual teeth or tusks; parrot fish have paired frontal teeth, top and bottom, fused into a parrot-like beak. Both have heavy pharyngeal teeth, which are powerful grinders, set well back in the throat. The wrasses are mostly elongated in body form and have a continuous dorsal fin. They are among the most common of the coral reef fish, swarming in and out of the caverns and grottoes which they frequent. As with the angel fish, wrasses can cause some confusion, for many species change greatly in both shape and coloration during growth; some even take on special nuptial colours in the breeding season.

An interesting story and one that illustrates how confusing these labrids can be, is told of *Lepidaplois albomaculatus*, once thought the rarest fish in the world. It was described as having, among other characteristics, a very distinctive pattern of large white spots on a jet black background. Such a strikingly marked species could surely not be mistaken for another. As the unique specimen was lost, the first published record was based on a painting made by the resident American Consul of Mauritius in about 1870.

For many years it was confidently believed to be a new species. No further specimen had been seen despite extensive search by underwater teams in the Indian Ocean. Then at long last, a skindiver who maintained a salt-water aquarium captured a similar example in Durban Harbour, South Africa, in 1962. Photographs of the fish were sent to the local ichthyologist, the late Professor J.L.B. Smith, for an opinion of its scientific value. Apparently it was greeted as the greatest find since the discovery of the coelacanth, a large prehistoric fish which in 1938 was found to be still in existence.

Although this newly discovered specimen died in its aquarium and was devoured by a hermit crab, others were soon caught in the same locality. One of these then revealed a most unexpected phenomenon. Within nine days the pattern and colour of the body underwent an unbelievable transformation, changing from black and white to golden brown with yellowish fins. This fish was thus proved to be one named *Lepidaplois axillaris*, a well-known and established species. So the mystery was solved. The 'rare' white-spotted fish was in fact merely a juvenile stage of *Lepidaplois axillaris*, and had inadvertently been given the name *Lepidaplois albomaculatus*.

The juvenile stages of this species are common in the region of the Capricorn Group of islands on the Great Barrier Reef. Usually seen singly frequenting the same locality, they are very inquisitive, active little fish and quite unafraid of divers. Occasionally they indulge in the habit of cleaning the bodies of other fish. I have observed them attending the spotted coral cod, *Cephalopholis miniatus,* and the larger coral trout, *Plectropoma maculatum,* picking off the many tiny parasites which find these slow-moving fish an easy target.

The largest of the labrids and the most magnificent to view underwater is the giant hump-headed maori wrasse, *Cheilinus undulatus.* This giant fish is coloured a beautiful green, and at the base of each of its large scales is a broad vertical bar of dark violet, bordered on each side with parallel orange lines. On the largest examples the scales sometimes measure five inches across. A pattern of wavy orange-yellow lines covers the whole of the head, resembling the tattoo marks on the face of a Maori. With age a big fleshy hump is developed on the head in advance of the eyes and one specimen captured in the Whitsunday Passage region of the Queensland coast measured seven and a half feet in length and weighted 420 pounds. Being a shy fish, the maori wrasse conceals itself in coral grottoes during the day, and begins to move about at sundown. Outside Australian waters it ranges widely throughout the coral reefs of the East Indies, the Red Sea and South Africa.

Among the sea basses and rock cods, Australian coral reefs have some of the loveliest species, including the very variable coral trout, the scarlet coral cod, the hump-backed cod, and the giant of them all, the Queensland groper. A characteristic of these fish is their large protractile mouth with protruding lower jaw. By habit they are carnivorous. Many reach a large size and almost all are excellent food fish. The Queensland groper, *Promicrops lanceolatus*, one of the largest fish in the Australian seas, is a wide-ranging species known to attain a length of ten feet. It has the reputation of being dangerous, and is said to be feared more than sharks by the divers of the pearl fleets. Modern skindivers hunt this huge fish and have successfully landed specimens over seven feet long and weighing 450 pounds.

My encounters with this species have forced me to the conclusion that it is a very curious but cautious fish. The number of coral reef dwellers it consumes must be enormous, and some fishermen contend that it eats the equivalent of its own body weight each day, but this is not so. One monster of over 400 pounds, speared off Wistari Reef in the Capricorn Group several years ago, regurgitated a cloud of partly digested coral cod, in all about ten pounds in weight. In addition there were numerous other fish in its stomach, including a relatively fresh reef shark three and a half feet long. However, a groper would not necessarily catch or be able to digest this amount of food every day.

Underwater observations of the feeding habits of this same giant groper have revealed that it does not rush at or chase its victims, but prefers to lurk in some deep cavern or grotto to await the arrival of unwary prey. Passing fish weighing several pounds, still swimming strongly but powerless to resist the tremendous suction, get drawn sideways into the groper's mouth.

Scattered throughout the coral reefs as well as the close inshore waters are the fish known to Americans as sea-perches or snappers. These handsome lutjanids (family Lutjanidae) comprise many species. Some grow to a large size and almost all of them are valuable food fish. Certain species however, are known to be poisonous, and if eaten can cause the tropical fish poisoning known as ciguatera. The origin of the poison has always been a mystery and details of how fish become affected are not fully known. It is thought to be through their feeding habits, with the poison probably originating in a blue-green alga. Weed eaters feeding on this accumulate it in their bodies. Carnivorous types feeding on these herbivorous fish also accumulate the poison within their muscles and tissues.

The toxic weed does not affect the fish, but humans eating one which contains a large amount of this toxin can be severely poisoned. Even though a fish of a certain species may have been eaten with perfect safety, other specimens of the same species may be dangerous on some other areas of reef where its eating habits may differ. Poisoning of this type is unpredictable, as the appearance of a fish's flesh gives no indication whatsoever as to whether poison is present or not, and as yet there is no simple chemical means of detecting it. Ordinary cooking procedures have no effect on the toxin. The chinaman fish, *Symphorus nematophorus*, and the red bass, *Lutjanus coatesi*, are two of those which have a reputation for being poisonous at times. Some fishermen say that they are never poisonous while others will have nothing to do with them. Nevertheless, because of the doubtful quality of the flesh, they are not accepted for sale at Government controlled fish markets or depots.

The symptoms of ciguatera are a tingling about the lips and tongue, and a feeling of numbness which may develop immediately or within thirty hours of ingestion. Sometimes this is followed by nausea, vomiting, abdominal pain and convulsions. In some cases sufferers complain that their teeth are loose, though they are actually as firm as ever. When victims survive after a severe attack, complete recovery is very slow and may take many months or even years.

On the other hand, the handsome red emperor, *Lutjanus sebae*, is one of the most sought after food fish of the coral reefs. The flesh is white, fine, delicately flavoured, altogether delicious, and should be cooked with care. The flesh of a large adult is just as tender as that of a young fish. A skindiver may often see the juvenile stage of the species, but the adult, which grows to a length of at least forty inches and weighs just under fifty pounds, is rarely seen. The reason is that skindivers tend to follow a reef's edge, working in comparatively shallow water, and so fail to encounter the adults which regularly frequent the much wider and deeper parts.

No single account could do justice to the vast and varied fish population of coral reefs. The enchanting beauty of the reef pools with their astonishingly abundant schools of gaily coloured, irridescent demoiselles, can be enjoyed by most visitors. Striking as these isolated surface scenes may be, by diving over the edge of a reef one can see at close quarters not only the smaller fish but also the numerous large and many-hued varieties which rarely remain in surface-level pools at low tide.

Underwater, the reef throbs with life. Brightly coloured fish flash by or hang motionless, while larger species swim past them with quiet deliberation. Amid the coral jungles flit wrasses, suspicious cod of many colours, and majestic, paired angel fish. The pastime of fish-watching is a revelation as fascinating in its variety as bird-watching although, unlike the latter, it is still in its infancy. To many people the idea of pursuing fish for any reason other than to haul them gasping out of the water on a hook or spear still seems strange. Wounded fish generally elicit scant sympathy for, unlike birds and mammals, they are cold-blooded and supposedly lack feeling. A short time spent fish-watching, however, helps to dispel this false idea and gains many converts.

The varied characteristics of the fish provide endless entertainment for those prepared to become acquainted with them. Where they are not continually harassed and frightened by spear-fishermen, fish are, like any other wild creatures, overcome by curiosity and soon come to rub noses with the skindiver. They quickly learn that they are safe and accept human intruders. If a diver works in the same locality for several days the fish may even pay him the supreme compliment of ignoring him.

Left: Regal Angel Fish, *Pygoplites diacanthus.* One of the most striking of the Angel Fish. This handsome specimen is photographed sixty feet deep off Wistari Reef. Angel Fish are readily distinguished from all other chaetodonts by the presence of the long stout preopercular spine readily observed on this specimen

Above: Imperial Angel Fish, *Pomacanthus imperator.* Exhibiting extremes of colour and contrast, this fish is not often seen among the corals of the Capricorn Group. Sykes Reef, thirty feet

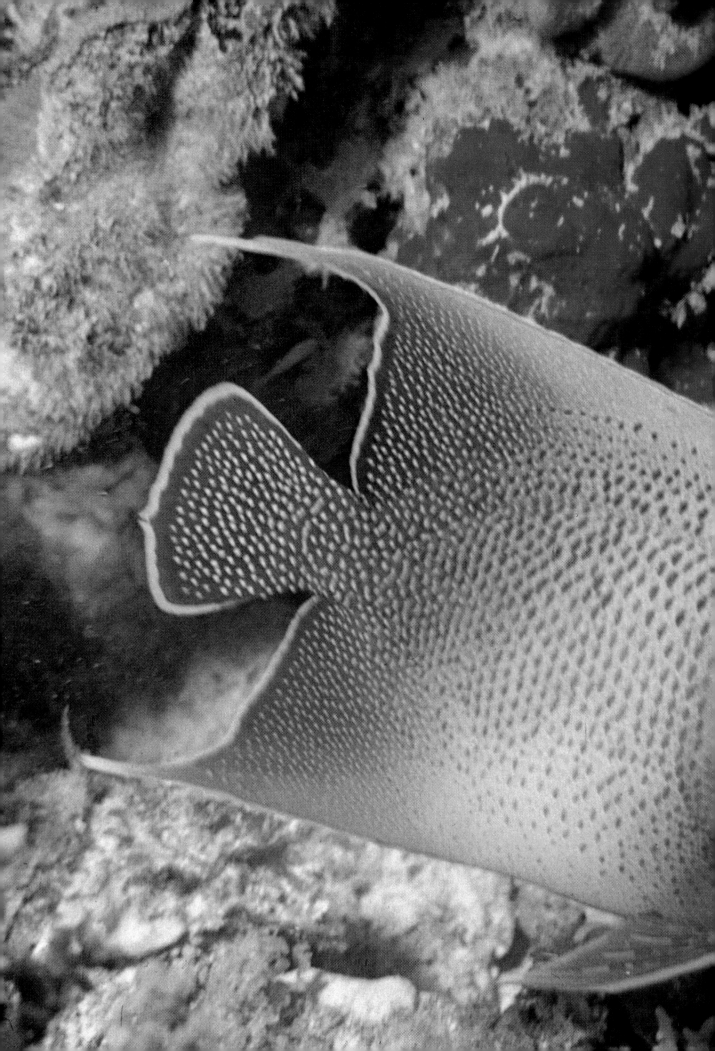

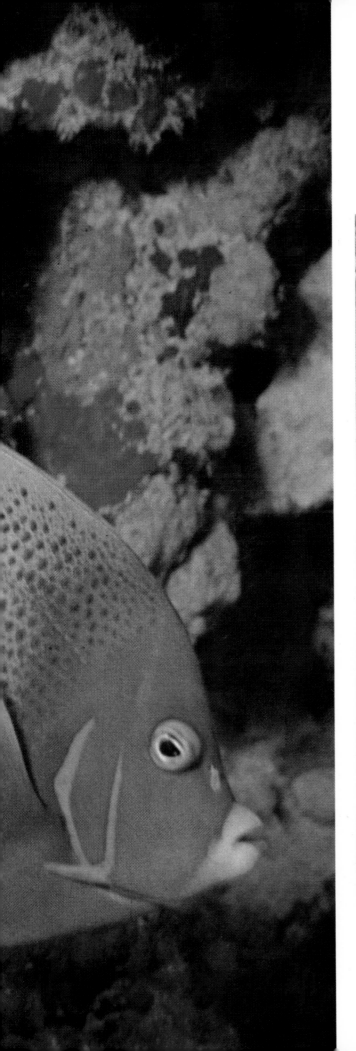

Zebra Angel Fish, *Pomacanthus semicirculatus.* Edged
with electric blue this fish is one of the most abundant
of the Angel Fish to be encountered throughout the
reef area

Left: Beaked Butterfly Fish, **Chelmon rostratus**, is
an excellent example of the elongated mouth developed
by some Butterfly Fish to probe for food among the
coral branches

Above left: Six-Banded Angel Fish, **Euxiphipops
sexstriatus,** is one of the larger Angel Fish occurring
in reef waters. Grows to twenty inches. Sykes Reef,
fifteen feet

Above right: Rainford's Butterfly Fish, **Chaetodon
rainfordi,** is very common among the coral growths.
Growing to five and a half inches, it is only known
to be found off the coast of Queensland. North-West
Island, fifteen feet

Left: Coral Trout, *Plectropoma maculatum*. One of the most sought after food fish of the reef area. Larger specimens often attain forty pounds in weight and over. This fish pictured here is at the entrance to its coral cave. Silver dashes in the background are schooling Pilchards. Wilson Island, sixty feet

Above: Black-Tipped Rock Cod, *Epinephelus faciatus*. One of the smaller and more colourful members of the wide-ranging genus of valuable food fishes. Wistari Reef, forty feet

Above: Spiny-Back Trumpet Fish, **Aulostomus chinensis.**
This two foot long fish varies in colour. Some are yellow
like the one pictured, while others are brown. Wistari
Reef, fifty feet

Right: Feather-Fin Bull Fish, **Heniochus acuminatus.**
A wide-ranging species, this fish has been recorded in
Queensland and occasionally reaches New South Wales.
The fourth dorsal spine is elongated into a long
filament-like pennant. Grows to ten inches. Wistari
Reef, thirty feet

Far right: Red Emperor, **Lutjanus sebae.** A handsome
fish which attains a weight of at least forty-five pounds
and a length of forty inches. It is one of the better
food fish of the reef. The fish illustrated here is in
the juvenile stage. Adult fish are salmon pink. North-
West Island

Above: A striking example of disruptive coloration, this two inch Dottyback *Pseudochromis sp.,* hovers close to its home, a hole in the coral 110 feet deep off Wistari Reef

Left: Silver Trevally, *Caranx nobilis.* One of the large Trevally which inhabit the warm waters of the reef and range from Central Queensland to the cooler southern states. North-West Island

Pages 40-41: Spotted Coral Cod, *Cephalopholis miniatus.* This colourful Rock Cod is sheltering under Plate Coral, one of its favourite haunts. This fish is often encountered among the corals of the Capricorns. Wistari Reef, forty feet

Left: Orange Sea Perches, *Anthias squammipinnis.*
These attractive little fish are commonly found inhabiting
the coral grottoes in deeper water

Above: Blue Puller, *Chromis caeruleus.* This brilliant
blue fish is found in large numbers, schooling among
the coral branches. Fish at left hand of picture can
be seen nestling between the coral growths, a favourite
protective measure adopted by these fish. Grows to
three inches. Yellow fish are juvenile chaetodonts

Pages 46-47: Yellow Emperor, *Diploprion bifasciatum.*
This fish is recorded found in India, China, Japan and
the East Indies, and grows to a length of twelve inches.
A common inhabitant of the coral caves of the Capricorns
this Yellow Emperor is hiding in its sponge and coral-
decorated retreat

Above: When they are not continually harried and
frightened by spear-fishermen, fish, like other wild
creatures, are soon overcome by curiosity and investigate
cameras and rub noses with the diver

Right: Fast-swimming Turrum *Caranx emburyi*, swim
in from the open sea to inspect divers. Known off the
Queensland coast as far south as the Capricorns, these
fish are terrific fighters on line or spear and spearmen
occasionally land specimens weighing up to eighty pounds

Above: Venus Tusk Fish, **Choerodon venustus.**
Commonly known to the fishermen of the Capricorns
and other northern reefs as the Blue Parrot, this
magnificent fish is one of the larger members of
the wrasses. The tusk-like canines in the front of
the jaws from which the fish take their name is well
displayed in this picture. Wistari Reef, sixty feet

Right above: Yellowtail Kingfish, **Seriola grandis.**
A large and powerful fish found in coastal and ocean
waters, the Yellowtail grows to a length of eight feet
and a weight of 150 pounds. Encountered commonly by
divers, they have the habit of circling the swimmer
once or twice before flashing away

Right below: Sheltering by a Porites Coral growth
these painted sweetlips **Spilotichthys pictus**, are
very common in Queensland waters. They are one of the
few fish that will let a diver approach close to them
before they swim away.

Pages 52-53: Orange Sea Perches, **Anthias squammipinnis.**
These attractive little fish are commonly found inhabiting
the coral grottoes in deeper water.

Far left: Once thought to be the rarest fish in the
world, this striking wrasse, *Lepidaplois axillaris*,
is a classic example of how confusing the various stages
of growth of the Labrids can be

Left and above: Cardinal Fish, *Apogon sp.* One
of the many variable little fish which inhabit the
coral growths. North-West Island, forty feet

Pages 54-55: Secure in its colourful home this Scarlet-
Fin Soldier Fish, *Holocentrus spinifer*, spends the
day waiting for nightfall when it will emerge and hunt
for food. These fish are armed with many spines and are
extremely rough to touch. This species is one of the
larger members of the family, and grows to fifteen inches
in length. Wistari Reef, seventy feet

Above: One of the more colourful members of its large family, the Blue-Banded Sea Perch, *Lutjanus Kasmira*, shelters among the branches of Staghorn Coral fifty feet deep on the slope of Wistari Reef

Right: Mangrove Jack, *Lutjanus argentimaculatus.* These fish seek the shelter of the coral caves during the day, emerging at dusk to commence feeding. Often confused with its close relative the Red Bass, *Lutjanus Coatesi*, the Mangrove Jack lacks the deep conspicuous pit in front of the eyes found on the Red Bass

ANEMONES
AND
ANEMONE FISH

ANEMONES AND ANEMONE FISH

Anyone who has walked the rocky seashores will be familiar with the sea-anemones. Flower-like in appearance and of many and varied colours, these often beautiful animals have attracted the attention of all who see them. Sea-anemones are a form of polyp, and like the corals belong to the Coelenterata division of animals, the other members of which also include the jellyfishes and the Portuguese man-of-war. All anemones are characterised by a lack of any respiratory or circulatory system. They have the ability to move their body parts muscularly and they possess stinging capsules used for offence or defence. Most of these anemones encountered on the Barrier Reef live in tidal pools. However, because of a remarkable capacity to withstand extremes of water temperature and pressure, they are found in most oceans and even inhabit the greater depths in regions of constant darkness.

The typical anemone has a cylindrical body fringed with translucent tentacles which surround a centrally situated mouth cavity located at the top. The anemone has no excretory system so the mouth serves both for ingestion and egestion. The animal clings to its chosen support by means of a sticky foot, and so tight is this hold it can rarely be dislodged without tearing. These sedentary creatures are capable of slow movement by means of a creeping action of the base and there are instances of anemones turning upside down and 'walking' on their tentacles. At least one species completely loosens its grip, slightly swells its body and gets carried along by the current. Sea-anemones are voracious carnivores and with the tentacles surrounding the mouth have an intricate and effective way of capturing prey. Similar to the corals, they are armed with stinging cell capsules that are invisible to the human eye. These cells are known as nematocysts and there are countless thousands of them embedded in the surface tissures of the tentacles and body walls. Each capsule contains an extremely small

coiled thread which is discharged instantaneously when pressure is applied to the trigger hair or cinidocil on the outside of the nematocyst's thin wall. Any small crustacean or fish unsuspectingly swimming within reach or brushing against some of the tentacles, touches hairs which immediately release thousands of stinging threads into its body, paralysing or killing it. The victim is then transferred from tentacle to tentacle until it reaches the mouth where it is drawn into the body of the anemone and digested.

Deadly and efficient as these tentacles are, some species of small, brightly-coloured fish associate with and live among the tentacles of certain giant tropical anemones. In the waters of the Great Barrier Reef, two genera, *Amphiprion* and *Premnas*, comprising about eight species of fish, live among the tentacles of several kinds of anemones. They are very much at home with their anemones and are able to touch the tentacles with perfect safety, rubbing against and burrowing into them. This association of free-living creatures for mutual benefit is known as commensalism, although in this case there appears to be a clear advantage to the fish.

Why the anemone fish is immune to the deadly tentacles is still a subject of controversy, and experiments have been made by many scentists to prove their various theories, many of which are contradictory. In aquariums some species of anemone fish have been found feeding upon the anemone's tentacles and the mucus which covers them. This has led to the belief that here may be the secret of the immunity. It has also been considered that the fish tame their anemone, but the popular though not wholly accepted theory is that the fish are covered by a special skin mucus which protects them against the deadly tentacles.

Anemone fish appear to pair off for life and in most species usually two fish are seen occupying an anemone,

sometimes with several young also present. Once a
pair have established a home in an anemone they will
jealously protect and vigorously maintain the territory
for themselves. They seldom swim more than a few feet
away from their anemone and when threatened with danger
quickly flee back among the mass of protective tentacles.
Then they cautiously peep out to survey the scene before
emerging once more and bustling busily about their
host.

Anemones may be seen without fish, but I have never
seen a fish of the genus *Amphiprion* swimming freely
or living among the coral without the protection of
an anemone. The slow, often gaudy fish must prove
easy prey without this protection and is probably
quickly eaten. In most species of anemone fish the
female outgrows the male in size and has been observed
to be the aggressive suitor. The male clears off an
area at the base of the anemone for the female to deposit
2—300 eggs. When laid, these are attended by both fish.
As with most marine life, details of the developing
young remain steeped in mystery but it is thought that
after hatching the young drift to the surface and feed
on plankton.

The tropical anemones with which these fish live in
such close contact are giants of their kind. They
can be seen in areas of coral, their tentacles
rippling like a field of wheat in the wind. A
changing current or swell 'blows' the tentacles
aside to reveal the colourful fish snuggling into
them.

Perhaps the most abundant anemone to be seen in Great
Barrier Reef waters is the brownish red *Physobrachia*,
nearly always found lodged among coral growths. The
elongated tentacles with their conspicuous lobed tips
protrude, while the main body column remains hidden from
sight. When disturbed sufficiently this anemone
retracts its tentacles and disappears from view deep
down into the coral. Towards evening the tentacles
of these large anemones progressively recede, finally
becoming almost hidden by the indrawing of some of the
upper body column, leaving them looking like great squat
tomatoes. A very early morning swim will reveal the
anemones still in this condition, so they appear to
shut up shop for the night. The anemone fish during
this period gets shut out and swims around the column
of its anemone. If deliberately pursued it will not
leave but will just place the anemone between itself
and its pursuer. It is difficult to see what benefit
the anemone derives from association with these fish.

In aquariums the fish has been known to drag food
scraps to its anemone, but in the natural habitat
large food scraps are scarce and this activity has
never been observed.

Below: Dusky Anemone Fish, *Amphiprion melanopus*,
nestling amongst the lobed tentacles of its anemone
Physobrachia. Usually found in pairs, the female grows
larger than the male. Wistari Reef, Capricorn Group,
thirty feet

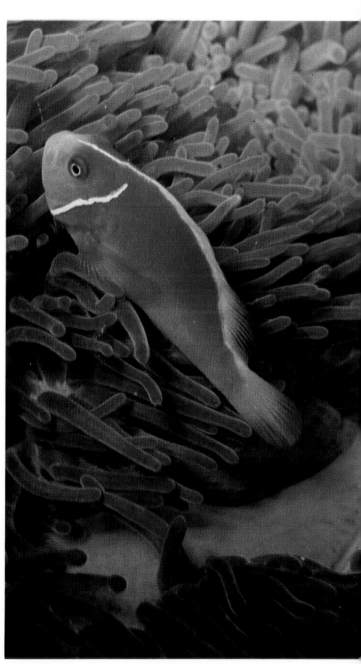

Above: Anemone Fish, *Amphiprion perideraion.* The pink column of the anemone can be seen just beneath the fish. Wistari Reef, thirty feet

Left: Yellow-Faced Anemone Fish, *Amphiprion unimaculatus*, one of the most common species amongst the corals of the Capricorn Group of islands. One Tree Island, fifty feet

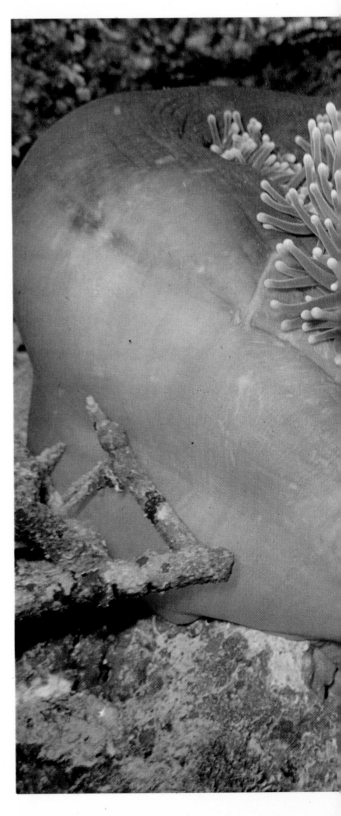

Above: Close-up of Yellow-Faced Anemone Fish showing how the fish nestles into, and actually comes into contact with, the anemone's tentacles. Wistari Reef, thirty feet

Right: Giant Tropical Anemone with tentacles contracted. As evening approaches the tentacles begin to recede progressively into the anemone

Far right: Anemone Fish, *Amphiprion perideraion*, hovering above the protective tentacles of their anemone

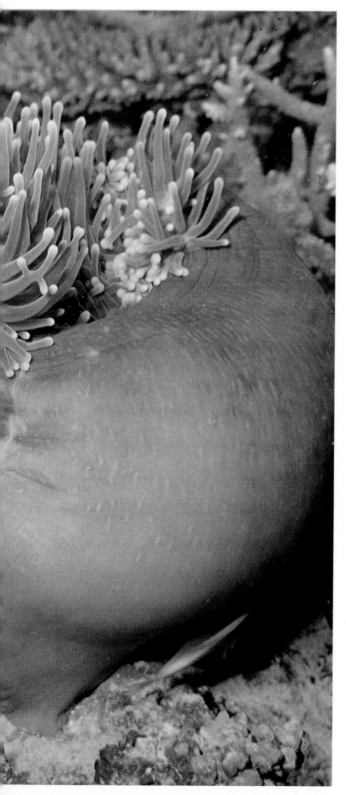
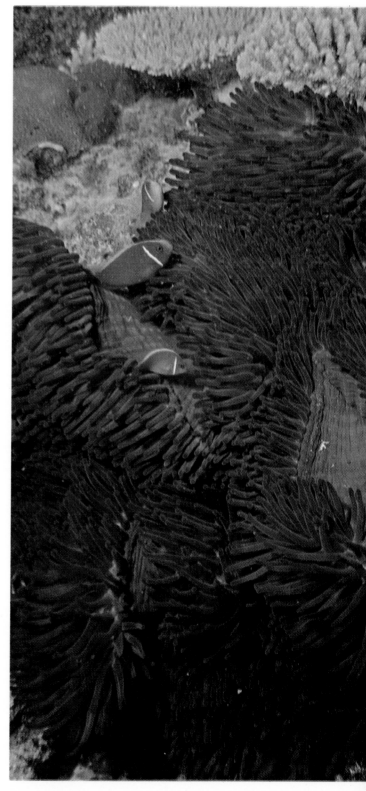

SHARKS AND
REMORAS

SHARKS AND REMORAS

At the mention of a shark, thanks to the tireless efforts of the popular Press, the average person visualises a vicious, razor-mouthed, man-eating monster of huge dimensions, bent on the destruction of some helpless human bather. The term man-eater is misleading as humans do not form the principal diet of any shark. All sharks are carnivorous, being predominantly eaters of fish including other sharks, although some of the smaller species feed on crustaceans, sea-urchins and worms. It is inconceivable to man, who preys unmercifully on all forms of life, that any of the so-called 'lower orders' should prey on him.

More than 250 species of shark exist, 100 different species being found in Australian waters, and very few of these could be considered harmful to man. The great majority are small crustacean-eaters, many less than three feet in length.

Sharks have been in existence for over 300 million years. Their body design has obviously been very successful for, compared with the bony fish, their form has not varied much during this time. Much is known of the life and breeding habits of the smaller cat sharks, of the family Orectolobidae, but the habits of larger sharks, the 'man-eaters' and typical sharks belonging to other families of the order Lamniformes, remain largely unknown. This is partly because some are wide-ranging pelagic species and, like many wild things, cannot endure captivity; but the chief reason is simply that there is very little profit in sharks, and research to enlarge knowledge takes a poor second place when the profit motive is absent.

Sharks differ from the bony fish in many interesting ways; the most important of these is the lack of true bones, the skeleton being composed of cartilage or gristle. There are several gill slits on each side of the head, usually five but sometimes six or seven, and the nostrils, used only for smelling as distinct from breathing, face downwards. Sharks breathe by taking into the mouth water which then passes over the gills and is ejected through the gill slits. In some species, the water is taken in through the spiracle, a hole just behind the eye. Sharks lack true scales of the type found in bony fish. Instead they have a tough abrasive skin called shagreen, covered with plate-like scales of hard bone or tooth-like structures called denticles. These minute denticles of the skin become greatly enlarged in the shark's mouth to form teeth. Unlike the teeth of other creatures, which are deeply rooted in sockets, they are simply embedded in the gums and connected to the jaws by fibrous tissue. Constantly replaced from inside the jaws as the functional teeth on the outer edge are broken, the varied forms of teeth of different sharks are an important factor in their classification.

Some harmless species have crushing plates adapted to eating crustaceans and sea-urchins, while the dangerous sharks have large, sharp, sometimes curved and often serrated teeth ideally suited to seizing and holding large prey. The teeth have been used by many indigenous peoples for weapons and ornaments, the Maoris greatly prizing those of the blue pointer, *Isurus glaucus*.

In sharks some senses are remarkably developed. They can smell, see, hear, taste and feel in the water, though their sight is reputedly imperfect. This may not be true, for their eyes are well developed and no doubt are quite efficient in an environment where views are very limited. Their sense of smell is very powerful and is their chief method of locating food.

An incident demonstrating just how much sharks rely on their sense of smell was the spearing of a large yellow-tail kingfish, which proved too strong for the spear-fisherman. As the nylon spear lines would not break the speargun had to be released. Off went the kingfish in a series of circles and dives, attempting to dislodge the spear protruding from its back. While the kingfish was still in sight a large whaler shark arrived at the scene and surprised us by swimming around in apparently aimless circles, instead of making straight for the wounded fish. We soon realised that the shark was following its nose, tracing every manoeuvre the fighting kingfish had made. At this stage the fish had disappeared but the shark eventually set off in the right direction and soon afterwards the sound of a spear rattling on the rocky bottom told us that the shark had slowly but surely tracked down its prey.

There is a line along the side of the shark's body, known as the lateral line, which is sensitive to low-frequency vibrations and plays a big part in helping it to locate its prey. Sharks can appear almost immediately a fish has been speared, and the blood, not having spread, could not be the cause of attraction. In the case just described, obviously the vibrations of the fighting fish had initially attracted the shark, bringing it to the scene where its sense of smell could take over.

The snout of a shark is covered by numerous small pores, called the Ampullae of Lorenzini, which are sensitive to temperature. The organs of hearing are entirely internal and give the shark a sense of position and balance.

Sharks are beautifully adapted to their environment and their magnificent streamlined bodies are a source of admiration to all who see them in their natural habitat. Lacking the swim bladders found in bony fish, sharks must keep moving in order to stay afloat. The tail, characteristically tilted up at an angle to the body, usually has an upper lobe much longer than the lower. Called the 'Heterocercal tail', this type of tail is ideal for cruising and gives the shark 'lift'.

In the pelagic or wandering sharks such as the blue pointer and white shark, these lobes are of almost equal size and shape. A tail of this type designates a speedy swimmer. The pelagic sharks are also equipped with two high, raised keels, one on each side of the tail-shaft. These and the pectoral fins prevent the torpedo-shaped body from rolling as the shark pursues fast prey.

Divers who have been lucky enough to see one of these monsters in the water have been overawed by their speed and form. The blue pointer especially is a magnificent creature with its lively colouring of a beautiful deep blue, its large lustrous eyes, sharp pointed snout and sleek, streamlined body that seems to quiver with muscular power.

As in the great dinosaurs of prehistoric times, the brain of a shark is tiny in contrast to the length and bulk attained by some species, and most of its area is concerned with the sense of smell.

The cat sharks are small species which live on the sea bottom and eat crustaceans and other small creatures. The two dorsal fins of these sluggish bottom-dwellers are of equal size and are placed farther down the back. The lower lobe of the tail is very poorly developed and the spiracles or breathing-vents are often large. There are five gill slits on each side. The cat sharks' colouring is usually brown or ochre, with white, black or rust-coloured spots scattered over the body. One pretty little creature called the epaulette shark, *Hemiscyllium ocellatum*, has two large black spots above each pectoral fin. Common in the corals of the Great Barrier Reef, they may be seen hiding with their heads under coral ledges during the day. At dusk with an incoming tide they become active and begin groping about in search of food. These are harmless creatures and can be picked up with ease. Too often people kill them because they are so pathetically easy to catch.

Most cat sharks are oviparous, laying eggs formed of a horny substance called keratin. They vary in colour from brown to black. Oval or pear shaped, they are adorned with tendrils or horns which help to anchor the eggs to seaweed or some other support. Sea water enters the shell and bathes the embryo during development. The cat sharks lay only one pair of eggs at a time, one developing in each oviduct.

Wobbegong or carpet sharks are also bottom-dwellers but they grow much larger, usually five or six feet long, though specimens of ten feet have been recorded. They are noted for their beautiful colour patterns and the presence of curious weed-like growths decorating and hiding the mouth. Their colouring resembles a symmetrical carpet design in browns and greys, ornamented with large lighter spots with faint cross-bands. This subtle combination effectively conceals these sharks as they lie among the weeds and rocks in which they live. Their teeth are like fangs, well-developed and arranged in several layers in both jaws.

Wobbegongs are considered harmless if left unmolested. Since the rise in popularity of skindiving however, encounters and incidents with them have occured frequently. Although docile when lying concealed, they become very active if fish are speared in their vicinity, often snapping at and trying to remove the struggling fish from the spear. Divers, attempting to recover wounded fish that have holed up in a cave or crevice, have been bitten, and while instances like these are probably cases of a hand or arm being mistaken for a fish, deliberate, unprovoked attacks have also been experienced during the breeding season.

Several species of this shark may be seen on a coral reef, and one of these, the banded carpet shark, *Orectolobus ornatus*, reaching a length of seven feet, may be found lying in coral pools. A rather rarer species, not often encountered and then only by divers in deeper water, is the tasselled wobbegong, *Eucrossorhinus ogilbyi.* Usually light in colour it has a remarkable profusion of branched and tassel-like skin flaps over the mouth. Many carpet sharks are ovo-viviparous, meaning that the eggs hatch out in the female's body, and the babies are born well-developed miniatures of the parents.

Many other species of the typical sharks are ovo-viviparous, but are in general larger, faster swimmers, well equipped with efficient teeth. Some of them are potentially dangerous to man. In contrast to the bottom-dwellers, the colour of these sharks is almost always plain, varying in shades of brown, grey or blue, with the under-surface usually a contrasting white. Colouring of this type occurs in many fishes and it serves two purposes. If viewed out of water when uniformly illuminated, the dark dorsal surface and light under-side make the shark two-toned and conspicuous. When in the sea however, a shark viewed from above blends with the dark sea bed, while from below its white belly appears to blend with the surface. A large shark swimming in deep water and viewed from the side should be a very conspicuous object, but the darker back is illuminated from the surface while the white belly is thrown into shadow. With this combination of top lighting and counter-shading the shark appears flat, dull and inconspicuous, blending perfectly with its background. This is called

obliterative coloration. Instances where large sharks have just materialised beside divers, seemingly appearing from nowhere, are due to this very efficient colouring.

One of the largest and the most ferocious of all sharks is undoubtedly the white pointer or white shark, *Carcharodon carcharias.* The longest white pointers recorded are thirty-six feet long, although they appear to be rare over fifteen feet. However, one specimen caught in Cuba was twenty-one feet in length and weighed 7,302 pounds. The white pointer's great body is designed for speed and it can swim even faster than the dolphin. The large, straight triangular teeth, with edges coarsely serrated, are perfectly designed for grasping and cutting up large prey. This shark has recently been responsible for several attacks on skindivers, particularly in South Australian waters, though the species is so wide-ranging that it can be found in the warmth of the tropics or the cold waters near the Arctic Ocean and Antarctica. Unlike most other large species, which are timid and cautious when approaching objects strange to them and will circle to look the possible victim over, the white pointer usually streaks straight into the attack. To this shark, accustomed to killing large prey like turtles, dolphins and seals, such a tactic is the most effective, and a skindiver, complete with wetsuit, could resemble a seal under water. It is interesting that these attacks have led to fewer fatalities among skindivers, than among bathers. In the past few years there has been an increase in the number of attacks by the white pointer on skindivers, who swim in deeper water and farther offshore than bathers. The skindiver though, is not swimming 'blind' like the bather. Therefore, even though he may know nothing until he feels the first heavy blow, he can (if not bitten clean in half, as one skindiver recently was) at least see what has hit him. He is usually armed, and is also conditioned to the possibility that he may some day be attacked, which makes him not as susceptible to shock at the horror of it and thus in a better position to fight back. Fortunately, large predators such as these are comparatively rare because their normal life span being long, their breeding rate is consequently slow.

Another species very dangerous to man, and a proven attacker, is the whaler, *Carcharhinus.* Their colour is very variable, ranging from light bronze to blue-black, often according to their locality, and they grow to twelve feet long. They are bottom-feeders, and are usually seen gliding along between the coral boulders. The name whaler originates from the early days of the whale industry when these sharks were numerous around the many dead whales. These are the dangerous sharks most likely to be encountered by visitors to the coral reef. They can be seen quite frequently, particularly during the warmer months, and some are about ten feet long. It is foolhardy to swim in the lagoons of the reef at dusk during this time of year, for these sharks come in over the reef and patrol the shallows for food at only a very short distance, perhaps three or four feet, from the water's edge.

Another large dangerous shark found on coral reefs is the tiger shark, *Galeocerdo cuvieri*. This blunt-headed shark with its characteristic tiger-stripe markings attains a length of sixteen feet and is a voracious feeder. A very prolific breeder, the female tiger shark can bear thirty to fifty baby sharks at one time.

I witnessed an eleven-foot female of this species attack a wounded eagle ray, *Aetobatus narinari*, at Sykes Reef in the Capricorn Group. The shark attacked with great force and ferocity and bit two large pieces out of the ray. As the shark turned for a third pass at the ray one of the skindivers hit it on the spine with an explosive power-head, killing it. When the two pieces of ray were removed from the dead shark the larger piece was found to weigh fifteen pounds.

These sharks are both prudent and very sure of themselves; masters of their environment, they should be treated with the utmost respect. Even very experienced skindivers choose to leave the water on the appearance of a large tiger shark. Nevertheless, the illusion prevalent among many people that tropical waters are inhabited by myriads of huge sharks, and that anyone luckless enough to fall overboard is invariably eaten, is the result of misinformation. Very few large sharks are encountered by skindivers. This is not to say that they are not there, but the rare encounters usually occur when fish have been speared, or when a large fish, wounded, has torn off the spear and holed up under a coral ledge. Even then the shark ignores the skindiver and concentrates on the fish. The large sharks mentioned have been proved dangerous and every encounter has an element of risk, but exaggerated fear of these creatures has arisen mainly from misinformation and lack of understanding.

Although rare in Queensland and never encountered in Great Barrier Reef waters, the much maligned grey nurse shark, *Carcharias arenarius*, deserves a mention here. When viewed underwater a shark is easy to identify, but if seen from land, during an attack for instance, correct indentification is almost impossible. This has led to misunderstanding on an unprecedented scale; people have assumed that any shark which appears to be grey is a grey nurse. Skindivers, either through ignorance or the wish to become the centre of attention, have been killing this shark in great numbers over the past few years. Experienced skindivers, however, are convinced that this docile, sluggish shark, which spends the day lying almost motionless in schools off rocky headlands or in sandy gutters, is, despite its impressive array of curved needle-like teeth, quite harmless to man. It is a heavy, flabby shark of stockier build than the faster, dangerous sharks, with the teeth of a fish-eater which are not designed for grasping large prey. In fact, there is no reliable record of an attack by the grey nurse on any human victim.

A robust, vividly marked, harmless shark inhabiting tropical coral reefs is the round-nosed, black tipped shark, *Carcharhinus melanopterus*. It is most often seen, in its haste to feed, almost climbing up over the reef with the incoming tide, when there is at first barely enough water to swim in. Similar to the whaler in shape, these sharks frequently frighten newcomers to the reefs, but the black-tipped fins and tail-fluke or lobe make them easy to identify.

A strange companion of sharks, the remora or suckerfish has the extraordinary habit of attaching itself to a shark by means of a powerful sucking disc occupying the whole of the top of the head. This is a peculiar modification of the dorsal fin which takes the form of flat plates or slats. By means of this structure the fish is able to attach itself to its chosen host. The advantages of this are twofold, the remora achieving both effortless transportation and a share in the host's meals. The suckerfish is not a parasite and does not harm its host in any way. It is a swift, powerful swimmer and quite capable of fending for itself when it chooses. It is not uncommon to observe one or two of the larger slender suckerfish, *Echeneis naucrates*, swimming about actively by themselves, and often a skindiver is approached and annoyed by one of these fish attempting to hitch a free ride.

When attaching itself, the slight raising of the plates creates a series of vacuum chambers, forming an extremely powerful attachment. The remora can free itself without effort by swimming forwards, thus lowering the plates and breaking the vacuum.

Remoras have been used by many fishermen of the Indo-Pacific as a means of catching turtles. The ingenious method was to fasten a light strong line securely above the tail of the fish and then to put to sea in canoes. When the quarry was sighted, the suckerfish, which was being carried either in or adhering to the bottom of the canoe, was pulled off and thrown towards the turtle. When the fish attached itself to the turtle the line was kept taut, making it impossible for the fish to release its hold.

The fish used for this purpose was the larger slender suckerfish which grows to thirty-eight inches in length.

Another species, the short suckerfish, *Remora remora*, is a shorter more thick-set fish which grows to only eighteen inches in length and is not seen as often as the larger species. I have never observed any swimming freely by themselves; usually they are seen clustered around the gills and pectoral fins of large sharks. Suckerfish are not particular about what they attach themselves to, and if a suitable host cannot be found then the bottom of a launch or fishing boat will do just as well.

Right: One of the most attractive of the cat sharks, this Epaulette Shark, *Hemiscyllium ocellatum*, grows to about two and a half feet and is quite harmless. North-West Island

Far right: Tasselled Wobbegong, *Eucrossorhinus ogilbyi*, is a tropical reef dweller, and is lighter in colour and differs in pattern from the more common Banded Carpet Shark. The Tasselled Wobbegong is readily distinguished by the profusion of curious weed-like growths around the mouth. Wistari Reef, Capricorn Group, fifty feet

Left: Merging perfectly with the growths on the sea bed among which it lies, this Banded Carpet Shark, *Orectolobus ornatus*, can become a nuisance when it snaps at divers. Although this particular shark was photographed in New South Wales, the Banded Carpet Sharks are wide ranging, and are also found in Queensland and Victoria. Bass Point, New South Wales, 125 feet

Above: Remains of a large Beaked Eagle Ray, *Aetobatus narinari*, after attack by a large Tiger Shark. Two pieces were taken, the largest weighing fifteen pounds

Above: Slender Sucker Fish, *Echeneis naucrates*, is often a companion of sharks as well as turtles and rays. There are several species in Great Barrier Reef waters and two of these are common. The Slender Sucker Fish pictured clinging to the bottom of a fishing boat is the largest of the species and reaches a length of thirty-eight inches

Right: Tiger Shark, *Galeocerdo cuvieri*. The wide, crescent-shaped jaws of this shark were responsible for the terrible wounds inflicted on the Eagle Ray. The victim's tail can still be seen protruding from its mouth. Sykes Reef, twenty feet

FISH
CLEANERS

FISH CLEANERS

Among the many curious relationships which exist between fish of different species, one of the strangest is known as 'cleaner' behaviour. Certain small fish obtain their food by picking parasites off the scales and skin of larger fish, and they may even enter the mouth or gills of the fish for this purpose. Some species of butterfly fish, gobies and wrasses have been observed occasionally cleaning other fish, but one pretty little fish, common on the Great Barrier Reef, sometimes establishes itself in a particular spot, and fish ranging from demoiselles to great manta rays will come to it periodically to be cleaned. Divers recognise these localities and call them cleaner stations. This interesting little fish a small species of wrasse called the blue streak, *Labroides dimidiatus* is a brilliant blue with a black longitudinal band which extends from the snout through the eye to the end of the tail or caudal fin. Reaching a length of four inches, this extremely active little creature moves very quickly when attending its clients, busily searching the surface area of the host for adhering parasites. Several cleaner fish may frequent the same cleaning station, which is usually a large coral boulder surrounded by sand or a conspicuous sandy gutter. Two or three fish of different species may be seen in the process of being cleaned at the same time.

I have observed this particular activity over a period of many months, and I have found that the behaviour of the cleaners and the fish coming to be cleaned follows a relatively set pattern. On arrival, a client will pause and wait for the attention of the cleaner, which rushes up and does a little dance around it. The client fish quite often visibly changes colour as if advertising its willingness to be cleaned. The coral trout, *Plectroploma maculatum*, is usually pinkish brown, liberally scattered with small blue spots, but when attended by a cleaner, it sometimes turns light grey with darker grey bands. I once watched a small school of black-tipped fusiliers, *Caesio chrysozonus*, hanging motionless near the bottom at a cleaner station. When approached by a cleaner fish one of the school changed colour, becoming much darker, and this was the only fish to be cleaned. The small cleaner darted away from the darker fish and nosed other members of the school but soon rushed back and resumed cleaning.

If business is slack and several wrasses are available, two or three can be seen attending the same fish. The fish waits patiently while its body is thoroughly cleaned and, should a fin be held tightly against the body, a few sharp nudges from the cleaner soon ensure that it is moved to facilitate thorough cleaning. As the gills are approached the client rolls on its side and extends one gill to be serviced. The cleaner pokes its head in under the gill plate, takes one or two tentative nibbles and, on sighting a parasite well established deep inside, disappears completely inside the flared gill cover. When this gill has been serviced the procedure is then repeated with the other.

Carnivorous fish like cod, with large protrudable mouths, open them wide and flare out both gill covers. The cleaners enter right into the mouth and sometimes make an exit through the gills. When the cod wants the cleaner to leave, it partly closes its mouth, then opens it wide again so that the tiny fish takes the hint and departs. I have gained the impression from observation that the client fish goes into a trance-like state and greatly enjoys the cleaning procedure. When the client feels it has had enough attention it changes back to its original colour, straightens up and becomes agitated. Should the cleaner fish persist, which it often does, it shrugs it off and swims away leaving the wrasse free to attend the next customer. Parrot fish are often observed with their head slightly inclined while their peculiar beak-like teeth are cleaned by several wrasses.

As always there is a villain ready to take advantage of any established behaviour. In this case the sabre-toothed blenny, *Aspidontis taeniatus,* a fish remarkably resembling the cleaner wrasse, frequents cleaner stations and goes through the same preliminary procedure as the cleaner wrasse to lure fish into believing they are about to be cleaned. However, after the initial dance, instead of picking off parasites it darts in and takes a lump out of the startled customer. Photographing this cleaner activity requires some patience, for after locating a cleaner station one must lie motionless for long periods, awaiting the arrival of clients. During this time I have received the undivided attention of several busy little cleaner wrasses, which have given me a thorough inspection from head to toe, but as rubber suits do not attract parasites they soon leave in disgust.

Right: Painted Sweetlips, *Spilotichthys pictus*, being attended by two cleaner fish

Above: Zebra Angel Fish, *Pomacanthus semicirculatus*, having its gills cleaned by Cleaner Wrasse, *Labroides dimidiatus.* With larger fish, the cleaner may enter right inside the gills

Right: Painted Sweetlips, *Spilotichthys pictus*, being attended by two cleaner fish

Above: Although it is a carnivorous species this Spiny-Backed Trumpet Fish, *Aulostomus chinensis*, does not harm the little cleaner fish

Right: Zebra Angel Fish, *Pomacanthus semicirculatus*, attended by Cleaner Wrasse, *Labroides dimidiatus*.

Far right: Sometimes the cleaner fish enters right into the mouth of larger fish in order to clean the inside of the gills

SPONGES

SPONGES

Living commonly on or among coral growths are a great variety of sponges (Porifera). They are among the most primitive of the reef fauna, being animals of a colonial type far less organised than are the corals. Sponges have existed much in their present state from early geological times, but it was not until the middle of the nineteenth century that they were accepted as animal rather than plant life. It has been estimated that more than 2,500 species inhabit the world's seas and they occur from the fringe of the shore to the deepest ocean abysses. As with some corals a certain confusion in classification is posed by the growth forms of similar species living in different environments. Quite apart from this there is the general marked diversity of the group as a whole and the great differences that exist in structural composition.

Some sponges are simple tube-like growths, while others resemble shrubs, fans or hands with numerous fingers. Individuals vary greatly from one to the other, both in their consistency and their colour. While some are tough or hard growths, often quite solid, others have a rubber-like resiliency, or else are truly spongy and quite easily compressed.

Apart from the damage done to the delicate tissues of certain sponges by slug-like molluscs called nudibranchs, the group can be said to enjoy marked immunity from attack or destruction. In fact, many sponges actually provide sanctuary and shelter for barnacles, small kinds of shelled molluscs and crabs.

On the Great Barrier Reef large vase-like or lettuce-shaped sponges occur over the flats exposed at low tide. Many of them are as much as twenty-four inches across and are brown or grey in colour. Other smaller kinds found inhabiting coral caverns and underwater outcrops are usually much brighter in colour ranging from blue and purple to red, orange and yellow.

The apparently slimy flesh of living sponges is comprised of countless simple forms of microscopic cells. These are assembled in a rather loose colonial arrangement and differ in character according to the function they perform. On the surface of a sponge are myriads of little pores which are the openings to an internal canal system. Water entering these pores brings food and oxygen to the interior of the growth, assisted by the beating of the whip-like tails of cells lining the canals. Finally the water and any waste is expelled through a number of comparatively large surface apertures.

The reproduction and development of sponges is similar to that of corals. Upon fertilisation of the ova, a free-swimming larva is produced. Sponges also reproduce by budding whereby a small protuberance grows into a new individual. This process increases the size of a sponge, and helps the regeneration of parts lost by damage or mutilation. Budding makes possible the cultivation of the commercial sponges. They can be cut into a small pieces which will grow to three times their size within eighteen months.

Although sponges are abundant on Australia's coral reefs, none of them is comparable in quality and texture to the overseas commercial varieties. Perhaps one day some limited industrial use will be made of one particular species; this is black in colour and grows to quite a large size in the deeper waters along the northern part of the Great Barrier Reef. Its internal skeleton or mesh is the typical horny, spongin composition, but this is a little too harsh for the more delicate uses to which commercial sponges are put.

Apart from the sponges with the typical spongin skeletal structure, there are numerous kinds with a calcareous framework. Others again that are normally found in deep ocean waters have skeleton composed of silica.

Right: This beautifully formed Cup Sponge grows on living coral

Below: Red Tube Sponge growing under a coral ledge ninety feet beneath the surface. Sponges feed by straining microscopic plants and animals from the water

Above: This large drab, vase-like sponge lives in the open water, and may measure several feet across

Left: The irregular shapes taken by many sponges make identification difficult. Water, drawn into the sponge through millions of microscopic pores on the outer surface, is passed through the body and expelled via large vents

Right: The orange and purple encrusting sponges add a splash of colour to this partially dead coral growth

MARINE
TURTLES

MARINE TURTLES

During the Triassic geologic period, when the ancestors of today's turtles first appeared, the majority were terrestrial and had already developed the characteristic shell and horny beak. Types evolved that could live in almost any environment and could subsist on anything from plants to prey. The fact that turtles have always retained some form of shell has ensured their survival for over 175 million years, and today modified versions are still worn by all species.

In sea turtles the shell has been lightened and reduced. The plastron, or lower shell, has a hinge running lengthwise, allowing the chest to expand and great quantities of air to be inhaled for prolonged diving. The feet have become flippers and are used more as wings than paddles, for turtles 'fly' through the water and are among the fastest of modern reptiles.

The only reptiles that give birth to live young are some lizards and snakes. Turtles and crocodiles produce eggs, another link with the land still kept by the sea turtle since the female comes ashore to lay.

Several species of turtles frequent Australia's coral reefs and three of these are abundant; the hawksbill or tortoise-shell turtle, *Eretmochelys imbricata*, the loggerhead, *Caretta caretta*, and the green or edible turtle, *Chelonia mydas*.

A once sought-after species is the striking carnivorous hawksbill. The heart-shaped shell, beautifully mottled brown and yellow, is the so-called tortoise-shell of commerce, which after the advent of plastics was no longer in demand. There has however, been an unexpected resurgence in the demand, perhaps because plastics have become too commonplace. The shields of the carapace are imbricated or overlapping like tiles on a roof, and the head is small with a hawk-like beak.

The loggerhead turtle is the bulkiest of the three. A carnivore, it lives on fish, has a pugnacious disposition when molested and is sometimes seen coming ashore to lay its eggs along with the green turtle.

The green turtle is the one most likely to be encountered by a visitor to a coral reef, and gets its name from the unusual green colour of its fat. A herbivorous species, it lives on seaweed growing on the coral reefs.

During the months of October and November, these turtles begin to gather in the warm, shallow waters of the southern islands of the Barrier Reef to breed. Mating takes place on the surface of the water and the fore flippers of the males are equipped with a single claw used to grasp the female during copulation, their longer tails also aiding in this task. Towards the end of October a few females may be seen awaiting the evening tide to begin the slow laborious journey up the open sands to the fringing vegetation to lay.

Their numbers continually increase until about mid-January, and by mid-February or thereabouts egg-laying ceases. A female may make this journey as many as seven times in a season, but not every female will necessarily lay every year.

Progression on land is an arduous task for the turtle—which weighs up to 400 pounds—as it is accustomed to having its bulk supported by the sea. With strong sweeps of the powerful front flippers and much heaving with the hind ones, the female lurches up the beach. After covering only a few feet at a time she usually rests before continuing the journey. The successive indentations made by the flippers resemble a tank track in the soft sand. The marks left by the tail indicate the direction in which the turtle has been heading, to or from the water. The tail leaves a broken line between the scalloped furrows formed by the flippers when the turtle climbs the sloping beach.

During the journey back to the water the tail drags to form an unbroken line in the sand. If disturbed on her way up the beach, the turtle makes desperate effort to swivel around and will return to the water. However, once she has selected a suitable site, one can approach and observe it from within a few feet. Either too exhausted or too intent upon egg-laying by this time, the turtle is oblivious of intruders.

With long sweeps of the front flippers the female turtle flings the sand aside to form a depression. When this is deep enough to accommodate her whole body the task of digging the egg pit is commenced. This hole is excavated with the hind flippers which scoop out a vertical pit with amazing dexterity. Digging is frequently interrupted while the turtle compresses the walls of the pit to prevent their collapse. Her task, which takes over an hour, is completed when the hole is as deep as the hind flippers can reach, usually about two feet. The eggs, which are white, and have a remarkable resemblance to a table-tennis ball, are then laid, slowly at first, but increasing to between twelve and fifteen a minute. Approximately 120 eggs may be laid at one time, although a range of 50 to 200 has been observed.

When the eggs are laid the nest is then filled in, the flippers again throwing sand in all directions, obliterating the position of the egg pit and making it difficult to know where the eggs are concealed. Thus the eggs have both warmth and safety during the period of incubation. The shell of the egg is like parchment, and if dropped will dent rather than break. Turtle eggs are peculiar, for when boiled the whites do not coagulate. Some inhabitants of tropical islands regard them as a delicacy.

As soon as the nest has been covered in, the turtle starts back for the sea. If she has by some chance missed the tide, she will have to lie stranded on the beach or reef throughout the day, enduring the heat of the sun until the incoming tide brings relief. The male green turtles never leave the water at this time. The females complete these labours unaided.

Once on land the marine turtle is a helpless creature and is often captured simply by being rolled over on to its back. Thus, with flippers vainly flailing, it can be kept for days before being cooked and eaten. Once, during a visit to a small uninhabited coral cay in the Capricorn Group, we came upon a large female turtle lying helpless on her back on the beach at the water's edge, in the fierce midday sun. Her mate swam to and fro, never leaving her but unable to assist and by the time she had been helped back into the water she was a very sick turtle indeed.

The complete egg-laying operation takes on the average two to three hours. The eggs, taking about ten weeks to hatch, are incubated by the heat of the sun and there is considerable wastage during this time as many eggs fail to hatch.

The newly hatched turtles are only about three inches long, and on emerging from the nest they instinctively head towards the water. Here they run the gauntlet of many eager predators. On land, these include birds by day and crabs by night, and for those reaching the sea there is no respite as reef sharks and other fish take their toll. With all these hazards it is not surprising that only a very small minority live to reach maturity.

Once in the sea, little is known of their life history thereafter, but the green turtle may travel distance of hundreds of miles in the open ocean. The turtles travel the same course over long stretches of open water which brings them eventually to that short stretch of beach which is the ancestral breeding ground, and where as adults they come ashore to lay.

It is not uncommon while skin-diving to find a turtle lying on the bottom or wedged under a coral ledge asleep, for during sleep the metabolism is so low that little oxygen is required. They may also be seen asleep on the surface of the water, being carried along by the current.

Excluding man, the green turtle, which is a powerful, graceful swimmer, has one principal enemy—the shark. A turtle may often be seen swimming by with part of or even a complete flipper missing. In the breeding season, divers are likely to receive some unwelcome attention from an over-amorous male turtle, and it can be hair-raising if, while absorbed in fish-watching or photography, one receives a gentle tap on the head, and on turning to investigate, finds the entire view blotted out by an enormous horny beak as wide as or wider than one's mask.

Green turtles were hunted commercially for their flesh and calipee (the gelatinous substance next to the lower shell) to make turtle soup, and factories were set up on several southern islands of the

Great Barrier Reef. Operating before the Second World War, only the females coming ashore to lay were taken. Little wonder that the turtle population was so reduced as to make it difficult to keep the operation going at a profit. Relics of one such factory can be seen rusting on North-West Island in the Capricorn Group. The taking of turtles or the collection of their eggs is now prohibited in Queensland, and the turtle industry there has ceased to exist.

Unhappily the future of the sea turtle is anything but assured, for not only is the hawksbill hunted again for tortoise-shell but all three species are now being killed in other parts of the world for calipee. Human ingenuity has discovered that excellent turtle soup can be made with any basic stock by using calipee alone to give the characteristic flavour. As a result, the carcass is left to rot. The calipee, when dried, can be stored indefinitely and transported from even the most isolated areas. So little is known of the migratory habits of sea turtles and so few breeding areas are protected (and even fewer policed) that it is doubtful whether their already reduced numbers can long survive the unchecked spread of this trade.

One way to preserve the green turtle would seem to be to farm the animal as an important source of human food, an animal which grazes on the abundant pastures of the sea and therefore does not compete with other animals grazing on land. There are many other reasons for saving the sea turtles—for the sheer delight of watching them fly through the water; so that one can stand on a quiet beach at dawn and see the females, their labours completed, return to the welcoming sea; so that one can witness the desperate dash of the newly hatched babies as they tumble over in their haste to reach the water; and because it is a sad thing when any species is driven to extinction by the greed or neglect of man.

Above: Green Turtle. If, after laying her eggs high up on the sand the female turtle misses the tide, she lies stranded in the heat of the day until the incoming tide brings relief. Her heavy bulk makes it impossible for her to struggle long distances on land. Fairfax Island

Right: Male Green Turtles are readily distinguished from females by their long tails. This one was asleep on the sandy bottom before being disturbed. Barnacles grow on his beak and shell. North-West Island, fifty feet

Above: Hawksbill Turtle, *Eretmochelys imbricata*, has a heart-shaped shell with the shields overlapping like shingles. These shingles are used for commercial tortoise-shell. This species is carnivorous and subsists on a diet of fish. North-West Island

Right: With a grace unknown on land, a Green Turtle, *Chelonia mydas*, 'flys' through the water with flippers poorly adapted for land use but skilful in the sea. Once hunted for their flesh to make soup, their slaughtering is now prohibited in Queensland and they are protected in Great Barrier Reef waters. One Tree Island. Capricorn Group

Far right: Female Green Turtles may attain a length of forty-eight inches and weigh up to 400 pounds. Males are only about two-thirds the size of the females. One Tree Island

THE
DANGEROUS
ONES

THE DANGEROUS ONES

Tropical reefs, for all their fragile beauty and lavish colour, always seem to have a price to exact of the careless intruder. When one thinks of danger in the sea, large predatory animals such as sharks immediately spring to mind, but although these may be dangerous, far more subtle sources of danger await to trap the unwary. The animals responsible for this insidious type of danger are of two distinct kinds—poisonous and venomous. They are poisonous when they produce toxic symptoms if eaten, and venomous when they produce noxious effects by means of stinging spines, stings or teeth.

There was no attempt to carry out intensive research into these dangers until the Second World War was extended to the Pacific area. Then, ironically, soldiers were issued with information enabling them to avoid dangerous marine animals while they continued to wipe each other out in numbers which must have been far in excess of all the victims of marine creatures throughout history.

Probably one of the first dangers made known to anyone visiting a coral reef is that of the consequences of treading on the dreaded stone fish. Because of their remarkable resemblance to a lump of stone or weathered coral, these fish do not swim away when approached but lie quite still, being practically indistinguishable from their surroundings. They lie under rocks or almost buried in sand and it is possible to walk on them or touch them with the hand while reefing. That squirming feeling underfoot is not necessarily a stone fish, for small flathead or flounder like to stay very still on the sandy bottom and are sometimes struggling underfoot before being noticed. An undignified leap into the air usually follows these encounters as one tends to expect the worst.

Stone fish occur throughout the Indo-Pacific in tropical reefs and estuaries. They are marine only, never having been recorded in fresh water, though they do enter river mouths. There are a number of different species, two of which are found in Australian waters. The most common, *Synanceja trachynis*, occurs right round the tropical coastline of Australia and grows to two feet in length, though the specimens found usually average ten inches. The skin is covered with a mass of warty excrescences, to which wisps of fine seaweed may be adhering. The skin, often beautiful, may be mottled green, reddish brown and yellow, but this is hidden under a thick layer of green slime. Usually the stone fish has thirteen dorsal spines, each provided with two venom glands hidden from sight in the enclosing tissue, a very thick layer of warty skin. Immediately the fish is disturbed, the spines, which normally lie flat, are raised rigidly erect and the slightest pressure causes the venom to flow swiftly along deep grooves to the tip of each spine. These are strong enough to go through the sole of an ordinary sandshoe, but although not rare, stone fish cause relatively few casualties. This is perhaps due to the fact that it is practically impossible to walk over the jagged obstacle course of an exposed reef without wearing strong, thick foot covering.

Even slight wounds inflicted by stone fish may be extremely painful and the effects can continue for several days. The pain of a deep wound is often so severe that the victim begins to thrash wildly, scream and finally lose consciousness. In some cases there may be complete paralysis of the injured limb, as well as nausea, vomiting, convulsions and eventually death. Recovery from a severe wound may take many months and the health of the victim may be permanently affected.

Scorpion fish, close relatives of the stone fish,

belong to a large group of carnivores which vary greatly in form. They do not grow to a very large size and are valuable food fishes. All have spines capable of stinging, but some species are extremely venomous and the pain is out of all-proportion to the insignificant nature of the wound. The family is widely distributed throughout all tropical seas. The bones of the head are characteristically spiny and some of them are beautifully coloured, often in a marble pattern which blends into the coloured sponges, weeds and corals among which they live. When taken from the water they have the habit of erecting the spiny dorsal fin and flaring out the armed gill covers. In spite of their impressive appearance the pectoral fins are unarmed. There are frequently twelve dorsal spines but sometimes thirteen or more. These fish can usually be distinguished from the more deadly stone fish which is scaleless and has thirteen spines. However a few species of scorpion fish are also scale-less, or the scales may be very small and embedded in the skin.

One of the most attractively coloured members of this family, the red scorpion fish, *Scorpaena cardinalis*, is highly valued as a food fish, its flesh being very white and tender. Like all scorpion fish it feeds on molluscs, crustaceans and small fish. The people most often stung by these fish are anglers attempting to remove them from the hook with their bare hands.

The beautiful butterfly cod, *Pterois volitans*, may be seen gracefully gliding among the corals of the Great Barrier Reef. Belonging to the same family, the fish is capable of inflicting a painful wound with its long, straight and slender spines. The body of this fantastic creature is usually only seven or eight inches long but the elongated dorsal and pectoral fins make it appear almost double its size. Camouflaged by these delicate lacy fins are the spines along which the venom grooves appear as deep channels, the glands being enveloped in a thin covering of skin. Specimens trapped in coral pools, feeling safe from aggressors, make no attempt to get away. As a result, this beautiful but slow-moving species is one of many being depleted at an alarming rate by those who trap them to sell to salt-water aquariums. A large percentage of them die en route to the nearest markets.

The tropical moray eels (Muraenidae) are ever-present inhabitants of coral reefs and often appear in the most unexpected places. These marine carnivores hide amid rocks and corals, twining their bodies into crevices in the reef. Morays are powerful and vicious biters and can inflict severe lacerations with their muscular, well-armed jaws. They like to hide in caves where they can lie in wait for prey, striking like a snake at anything swimming within reach. There are over 100 known species living in tropical and sub-tropical seas. The largest of these species, *Evenchelys macrurus*, grows to over twelve feet in length, and is found in Queensland waters. Identification can be difficult in some species because of great variation in colour and patterning. For example the Moray eel, *Gymnothorax Flavimarqinatus* a common though striking creature, is brownish grey, peppered with small black spots. It attains a length of four feet. Many divers fear the moray partly because, in order to breathe, it opens its mouth while gasping rhythmically in the water and so gives the impression of being about to attack. Although the moray will savage a hand or arm inadvertently placed in its crevice or cave, it very seldom attacks unless provoked.

Stingrays, close relatives of sharks, are common in tropical seas. They are often found partially buried in the sand with only their eyes and spiracles exposed, and although usually inactive they are capable of considerable speed. Stingrays are mostly ovo-viviparous, giving birth to tiny young which are perfect miniatures of the parents. Several families occur in Australia and two of these are well represented in the tropical waters of coral reefs.

Members of the family Dasyatidae are large and usually have a whip-tail with no dorsal or caudal fins. A well-developed spine located some distance from the base of the tail is an effective striking weapon apparently used for defensive purposes only. Species belonging to the family Urolophidae are smaller and have a thicker tail with a caudal fin and a long serrated spine at the base of the tail. The effectiveness of these spines varies according to the size and position on the tail, and although stingrays usually have the one spine, an individual may have two or three. For many years, there was some doubt as to whether the spine carried a poison. Later research revealed the presence of poison-secreting tissue in grooves along either edge of the spine, which produced poison of a virulent nature. Each side of the spine, which is composed of a hard bone-like substance called vasodentine, is armed with a series of sharp recurved teeth.

Wounds inflicted by stingrays are of a jagged or puncture type, and swelling accompanied by an irritating burning pain are the general symptoms. Application of heat will help alleviate the pain—from my own experience, I have found that a hot water bottle is ideal. As the wound is often a puncture everything possible should be done to avoid infection, which can cause complications.

The blue-spotted reef ray, *Taeniura lymma*, is a very pretty little ray and quite common in the sandy shallow lagoons of the Great Barrier Reef. Reddish tan in colour with large blue spots, it is often seen sending up puffs of sand when disturbed. One large ray, the thorny ray *Urogymnus africanus* possesses no poison spine at all. Instead the upper surface of the body and tail is heavily armed with sharp, thorny tubercles. The body is oval in outline and by comparison with other species of large ray, quite deep. The only time I have ever seen one of these curious rays was at dusk, forty feet deep over the reef edge of North-West Island, in the Capricorn Group. This particular specimen, which was at least six feet long, was busily puffing holes in the sand, then feeding on the worms and crustaceans that were uncovered. The thorny ray is widely distributed in tropical seas throughout the world, but, nevertheless, is rather rare in Australia and has only been recorded in Queensland waters.

Poisonous fishes are widely distributed throughout the world, particularly in tropical coral reefs. The family Tetraodontidae, to which the highly poisonous puffers and porcupine fish belong, is well known for its toxic qualities. The puffers or toadoes are fish of sluggish habits with scaleless and prickly skin and inflatable abdomens. Their fins are made up of soft rays only, without spines, and their jaws form a bony beak. These are among the most poisonous of all marine creatures and the liver, intestines and skin usually contain a powerful nerve poison which is tasteless, odourless and extremely poisonous. Most people living in the regions where this fish occurs are aware of its deadly poison but it is still eaten, particularly in Japan and the Philippines. Although careful attention is given to the removal of dangerous parts, the fish is still the cause of many fatal cases of food poisoning. The symptoms can develop within ten to forty minutes of ingestion. The victim experiences tingling of the lips, nausea, difficulty in swallowing, convulsions,

and in the worse cases death follows by respiratory paralysis.

During Captain Cook's voyage in the 'Resolution' there were two outbreaks of severe fish poisoning among the party. The first was the result of eating three fish of the species *Lutjanus bohar* which are similar to the red bass, *Lutjanus coatesi*. All who were affected eventually recovered but were very weak and ill for several weeks. The second instance involved Cook himself. Although he barely tasted part of the liver of a member of the deadly Tetraodontidae family he nevertheless experienced the first symptoms several hours later. Apart from experiencing numbness, nausea and difficulty in standing, Cook said he could not distinguish between light and heavy objects, for a pitcher full of water and a feather both felt the same to him.

An invertebrate that stings is the Hydroid *Lytocarpus philippinus*, a very fragile looking fern-like hydroid of great beauty. Found growing on rocks in plume-like tufts, this invertebrate is one of the most simple of Coelenterates, the Hydroza. A diver blundering into a large growth of these hydroids experiences much the same acute discomfort as that caused by falling into a clump of nettles. Thousands of minute stinging cells called nematocysts each charged with a little venom, are shot into the skin and break off there. Brushing against this animal can produce quite a numbing shock, especially if a large area of skin has been brought into contact with it. This hydroid may be encountered occasionally in the shallow coral pools exposed at low tide, but these scraggy specimens give no indication of the magnificent growths to be found in the deeper water beyond the reef's edge. To see this fluffy hydroid on a coral boulder in its natural habitat makes it difficult to recognise that a creature like a fern, attached to a rock, is in fact an animal. Only the sea with its vast profusion of roving plankton and organic life could nourish and sustain such stationary creatures.

My own experiences of poisonous or otherwise dangerous venomous creatures during many years diving, have been plentiful and varied and include being bitten by a toadfish, stung by a sea-urchin, having several pieces of flesh gouged out by a moray eel, and finding a large carpet shark determinedly fastened onto the end of a flipper.

The result of careless contact with the creatures described in this chapter may be terrible and painful.

However, it should be remembered that these poisoning processes have been envolved for the purpose of defence and food-gathering, to equip their owners for the relentless struggle for survival waged constantly by the inhabitants of the sea. Humans conditioned to leading a sheltered, protected life with few if any predators to fear, fall easy victims to the traps set in the jungles of a coral reef. However, in almost all cases where man has come off second best, he has been the aggressor.

Right: The delicate graceful fins of this Butterfly Cod, *Pteropterus antennata*, conceal long, sharp, venomous spines

Below: The deadly Stone Fish, *Synanceja trachynis*, lying on coral. This fish has been disturbed and has adopted the defensive measure of erecting its venomous spines. This one was found on the reef flat, and was, except for eyes and mouth, completely submerged in sand

Above left: This small Puffer Fish or Toado belongs to a family of deadly poisonous fish. The prickly skin, parrot beak-like teeth and inflatable abdomen, make them readily recognisable. These fish must never be eaten

Above right: Close-up of Stone Fish

Right: Close-up of *Lytocarpus philippinus*

Far right: This fern-like Hydroid, *Lytocarpus philippinus*, delicate and harmless as it may appear, is capable of delivering a nettle-like sting to any diver careless enough to brush against it

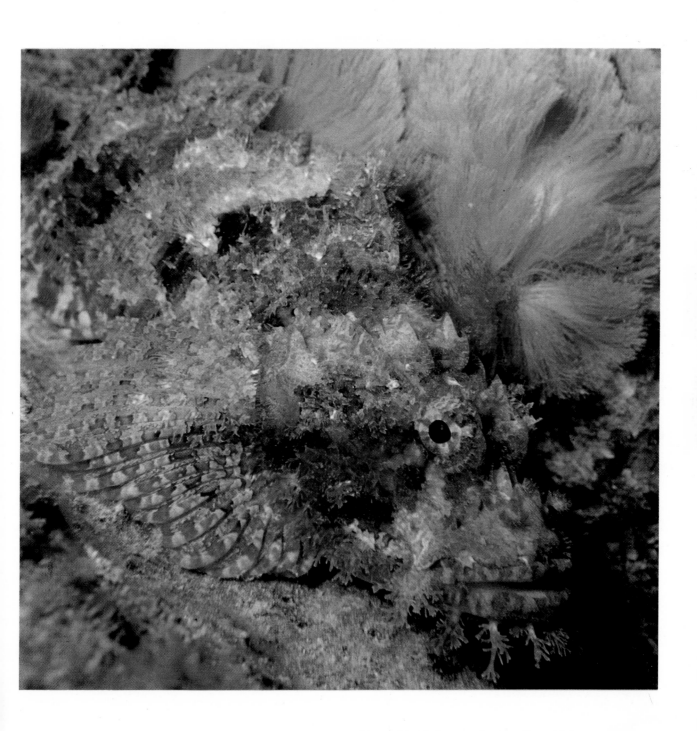

Left: Black Stingray, *Dasyatis brevicaudata*, is probably the largest of the world's stingrays, specimens of up to fourteen feet long and six and a half feet wide have been recorded. This example, six feet in length, lies on the sand forty feet deep off North-West Island, Capricorn Group

Above: Marbled patterning blending with its environment, this Scorpion Fish, *Scorpaenopsis*, lies in wait for prey. Camouflage like this makes it easy to accidently touch the venomous spines

Left: Moray Eels with their muscular, well-armed jaws are capable of inflicting serious wounds. This Moray Eel, *Gymnothorax flavimarginatus*; thrusts its serpent-like head out of its cave ninety-five feet deep off Wistari Reef

Above: This Thorny Ray, *Urogymnus africanus*, possesses no venomous spine on its tail, but is protected by sharp, spiny tubercles which cover the tail and upper surface of the body. North-West Island, forty feet deep

Left: One of the most beautifully marked stingrays of the Great Barrier Reef, this Blue-Spotted Reef Ray, *Taeniura lymma*, nestles among the coral growths. This stingray grows to three feet or more in length

Above: Duckbill Ray or Beaked Eagle Ray, *Aetobatus narinari*, is one of the larger rays of tropical and sub-tropical seas and feeds chiefly on molluscs which it crushes with its extraordinary, pavement-like teeth

SEA-STARS
AND
SEA-URCHINS

SEA-STARS AND SEA-URCHINS

Few people might realise that the brilliant sea-star they see lying in a coral pool is a close relative of that curious creature the sea-urchin, which dominates the same pool with its mass of needle-sharp spines.

Both belong to the unique group of invertebrates known as echinoderms, whose members include the feather stars, brittle stars and sea-cucumbers or trepang. All are encased in a tough covering, the name echinoderm being derived from the Greek echinas, a hedgehog and derma, the skin. Although there are wide variations of form between the various members of this family, all are united by the adults' radial symmetry and by the possession of tube feet.

Of the many varieties of sea-stars to be discovered on a coral reef the one most likely to attract the attention of fossickers would be the blue sea-star, *Linkia laevigata*. So brilliant is its colour and so boldly does it display itself that it is one of the most outstanding attractions of the reef flat. Unlike most sea-stars which seek shade and shelter, *Linkia* lies on the sandy bottom of coral pools in bright sunlight. So characteristic of the exposed reef are these sea-stars that one almost invariably appears in any photograph of a coral pool.

On picking up this striking sea-star, the first impression one gains is of the rigidity of the more or less cylindrical arms, which are not true appendages but actually form part of the body. The rigidity of the animal is mainly due to the presence of loosely-linked skeletal plates or ossicles which form a mosaic-like pavement just beneath the sea-star's skin. This pattern of movable plates allows the remarkable flexibility, however slow it may be, of the sea-star's arms. On the upper surface of the arms and disc are tiny, pincer-like, snapping organs called pedicellariae.

Commonly in the form of paired pincers, they lie in minute pockets in the surface and are continually opening and closing under muscular control. Their function is to police the upper surface, keeping small enemies and possibly debris off the body.

Together with the sea-urchins, sea-stars have the distinction of being the only animals in the world equipped with pedicellariae. On exposing the sea-star's under-surface each arm is seen to have a deep groove which radiates from the central mouth to the tip of each extremity. From these grooves numerous tiny, soft-walled projections may be seen weaving about. These are tube feet, operated by what is known as the water vascular system; they enable the sea-star to move about by the combination of muscular and hydraulic mechanisms. Sea water for this function is taken into the body through a special sieve plate situated on the upper surface and conveyed to the tube feet by a system of canals. In most sea-stars the tube feet are provided with special terminal suckers which can grip any surface with considerable force and make it possible for them to climb a vertical surface.

Specialised tube feet lacking suckers are found on the extremity of each arm. Very sensitive to vibrations and chemical substances in the water, their function is to feel the way and sense out danger as the animal moves over the sea bed. With the exception of a few deep-water species, each arm has also at its tip a small light-sensitive area that bears a cluster of simple eyes.

Most sea-stars prefer molluscs as food. Some prey on others of their own kind like sea-urchins and sea-cucumbers, while others filter mud for organic matter. Those whose favourite food is molluscs have become predators of bivalves such as mussels, clams and oysters. They lever the valves open by steady relentless suction of the tube feet until their protrudable stomachs can be inserted into the opening.

European oyster-farmers suffering the depredations of these creatures chopped them up and threw the pieces back into the sea. They soon ceased this practice when they learned of the regenerative powers of the sea-star. If any portion thrown back into the sea still had part of the central disc attached this would eventually grow into a fully-formed sea-star. Most are able to replace a lost arm and are frequently encountered in the process of regenerating a mutilated limb. The blue *Linkia*, together with other members of this genus, is the only one capable of reorganising itself into a complete sea-star from a small piece of arm with no part of the body disc attached. This blue sea-star is becoming increasingly rare on the more frequented Barrier Reef islands, as its vivid colour and the fact that it can easily be preserved make it a sure target for the many souvenir hunters.

One delicate long-armed sea-star, *Iconaster longimarius*, is never encountered on the reef flats. It inhabits the deeper water where only a skindiver can venture, living among the small clumps of coral on the sand. One of the smaller members, *Fromia elegans*, ranges from dark red to orange-red and is usually abundant on the exposed reef flats. It appears to require no specialised habitat however, as it may also be encountered on sandy patches, as well as clinging upside down to the roof of a colourful cave in deeper water.

While exploring the reef flats, one may overturn some coral boulders thus disturbing numerous creatures of infinite variety. One is likely to see some frenzied activity by a number of curious sea-stars with rapidly moving serpentine arms. Pick one of these up and it will probably snap off the whole or part of its arm. This delicate creature is aptly called a brittle star and is closely related to the large blue sea-star which is probably lying in a nearby coral pool. Brittle stars shun light however, and seek the shade and shelter offered by the underside of protective coral boulders.

Important changes occurred in part of the sea-star family many millions of years ago. The broad flat arms became long and thin and the skeletal plates were gradually rearranged. Along with these changes the body developed into a button-like disc. These modifications enabled the arms to be moved sinuously in the horizontal plane and resulted in the echinoderm known as the brittle star, *Ophiuroidea*. Since the arms can be bent they can be used for locomotion and this species can propel itself along much faster than the ordinary sea-star. There are no deep longitudinal grooves on the underside of the arms as there are in other sea-stars. They are practically solid. Tube feet are present but in this group they are almost always without suckers, although they still help in locomotion and also serve as respiratory and touch organs. Brittle stars do not hunt live prey, but filter sand and mud through the mouth, which is provided with tiny calcareous teeth. Decaying animal and vegetable matter is removed, then digested, and waste is egested through the mouth, the only opening.

Even more delicate in form, the crinoids or feather stars are not usually inhabitants of the exposed reef, preferring to live in deeper water beyond the reef edge. They are free-swimming animals which attach themselves by grasping rocks or coral with the whorls of jointed 'tendrils' on the underside of their cup-shaped bodies. The arms are like delicate fern fronds, in which the 'leaves' are spread out sideways to increase the area in which food can be caught. Each frond or arm has a groove which leads to the mouth at the centre of the upper surface of the body.

Many of these feather stars are to be seen, looking for all the world like lovely ferns. They frequent large caves and coral outcrops with arms outspread, catching food which drifts by in the current. One of the most amazing sights a diver is likely to witness is one of these feather stars releasing its grip on the reef, flapping numerous feathery arms and swimming off purposefully down a slope into deeper water. The creature is of course an animal, but the sight of something so obviously plant-like behaving as no plant ought to behave is quite startling.

Because many species are armed with long, needle-sharp spines, sea-urchins are undoubtedly the most feared of the echinoderms, and are the curse of reefer and skindiver alike. Although the familiar sea-urchin of the tidal pools is usually rounded in outline, other kinds assume many different shapes. The sand-dwellers especially have evolved a range so strange and varied that such names as sand dollar, cake urchin and heart urchin are used to describe them.

When a sea-urchin dies and the spines and flesh fall away, the limy test or shell remains. Unlike the sea-stars, whose plates are loosely linked, the shell of a sea-urchin is usually rigid. The regular symmetrical patterning of the plates and the exposed tubercles make the shell an object of beauty and a treasured find when washed up on the beach.

Sea-urchin spines are movable, each having a concave base which fits over a tubercle on the shell. Most species have long (primary) and short (secondary) spines among which are long slender tube feet. These tube feet can be observed constantly waving about, bending and straightening, extending and contracting, ever ready to detect the approach of food or enemies.

In most sea-urchins some of the tube feet support the weight of the body and, combined with movement of the lower spines, propel the animal forward. A few long-spined tropical kinds do not use tube feet for locomotion but walk on the tips of the spines. Progress is quite rapid and is made by co-ordinated movement of the spines working on their ball-and-socket joints. One of the long-spined varieties presents a fascinating spectacle when moving over the reef. The mass of long needle-sharp spines are constantly weaving about quite independently of each other, changing direction, forever constantly readjusting themselves to suit the movement and position of the sea-urchin.

Small jaw-like pedicellariae on long flexible stalks are also present among the spines, and as they have several duties to perform, as many as four kinds may be found on some sea-urchins. One of their primary functions is defence; when a foreign body comes into contact with the pedicellariae it is immediately seized and the hold is not released as long as the object still moves. Should the creature they are holding be too strong, the pedicellariae will not release this grip even though they may be torn from the sea-urchin's body. Others assist in procuring food which they seize and pass from jaw to jaw until it reaches the mouth, while even more specialised pedicellariae are equipped with venom glands capable of producing toxic material.

The sea-urchin is capable of chewing food so it does not extend its stomach outside its body to envelop prey as do the sea-stars. Most sea-urchins are herbivorous but some get nutriment from organic matter found in mud and sand.

The most striking sea-urchin to be found on the Barrier Reef, *Diadema setosum*, has five jewel-like spots on its casing, and is equipped with exceptionally long, slender and very sharp spines. These are kept in constant motion and may be a foot long in large specimens. They are extremely fragile, so the slightest contact will cause the spines to penetrate quite deeply and break off in the flesh. They are hollow, and once embedded in tissue are very difficult to remove due to whorls of minute teeth around each spine that resist extraction. They crumble easily when attempts are made to remove them with tweezers.

The slate-pencil urchin, *Heterocentrotus mamillatus*, has spines completely different from those of *Diadema setosum*. They may grow to five inches in length and half an inch thick and resemble thick, coloured crayons. It is quite obvious that the spines of this type could not possibly puncture flesh but this species should, nevertheless, be handled with caution since it has well-developed venomous pedicellariae.

A little sea-urchin found in large numbers, *Echinometra mathaei*, bores into pockets under coral boulders. The species varies in colour from olive green to a pinkish hue, often with the short, robust spines tipped with white. These sea-urchins are sometimes found fitting so closely into rounded spherical hollows of hard rock that one wonders how they can extricate themselves. These hollows have aroused great interest, and there is some conjecture as to how the sea-urchins manage to erode so much rock. But the conclusion is that the spines, by constant rotation and rubbing, wear the rock away. The teeth also play a prominent part.

Some species may be seen in exposed areas looking rather ludicrous, adorned with all kinds of paraphernalia from the sea bed. Mussel shells, oyster shells, bits of seaweed and many other unidentifiable objects form what appears to be a pathetic attempt at camouflage. The entire collection is held in place by the tube feet, each piece arranged so that it will provide maximum coverage. It is however, the means adopted by the sea-urchin to protect itself from too much light, and not an attempt at camouflage.

* Long-Armed Sea-Star, *Iconaster longimarius (moebus).*
This elegant species inhabits deeper water and is found
on sand or small coral clumps. North-West Island, sixty
feet

* Above: Biscuit Star, **Pentagonaster sp.** A small sea-star found living among the coral growths in deeper water. North-West Island, sixty feet

* Left: Sea-Star, **Ferdina ocellata**, resting among the corals. A shallow water inhabitant, it frequents the reef slopes below the low tide level. North-West Island, fifteen feet

Far left: One of the smaller sea-stars of the reef, **Fromia elegans**, clings tenaciously by suckered tube feet to the colourful sponge-covered roof of a coral grotto. North-West Island, forty feet

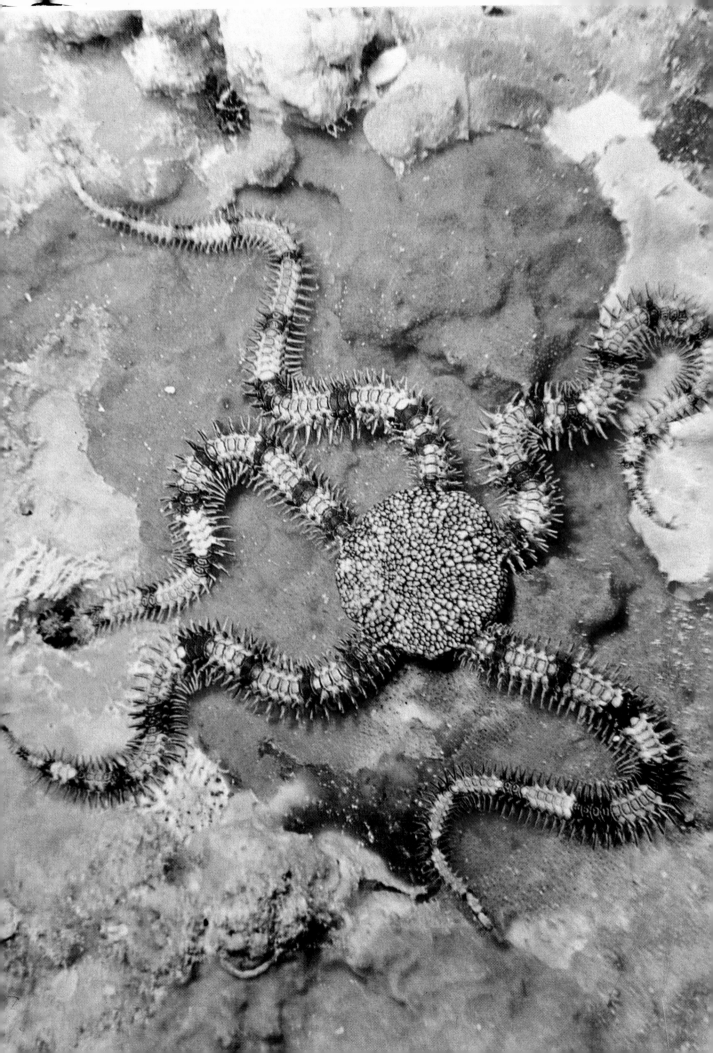

Above: This delicate, graceful Brittle Star, *Ophiocoma imbricatus*, is found under boulders on the reef flat. Brittle Stars do not like light, and seek the shade and protection offered by such shelter

Far left: One of the most common sea-stars found beneath coral boulders. This Brittle Star, *Ophiocoma insularia* variety *Variegata*, is crawling on the underside of a recently overturned boulder

Left: One of the larger and more conspicious sea-stars of the Great Barrier Reef, the cobalt Blue Linkia grows to twelve inches. Unlike most sea-stars Linkia lies exposed in bright sunlight

Above: Resembling a delicate fern, this Feather Star, *Crinoidea*, attaches itself to the reef by jointed cirri which are clearly seen in this photograph

Right: Long-Spine Sea-Urchin, *Diadema setosum.* One of the larger sea-urchins on the Barrier Reef, with long needle-like spines which penetrate flesh and break off. Whorls of tiny teeth on the spines make extraction difficult

* Above: Often found fitting tightly into pockets under coral, the Little Sea-Urchin, *Echinometra mathaei*, varies in colour from olive green to a pinkish hue

Right: Long Spine Sea-Urchin, *Diadema setosum*. The most striking Sea-Urchin to be found on the Barrier Reef. They are equipped with long, slender and very sharp spines

* Far right: Slate-Pencil Urchin, *Heterocentrotus mamillatus*, has heavy spines resembling thick-coloured crayons. This sea-urchin is well equipped for defence with developed, venomous pedicellariae

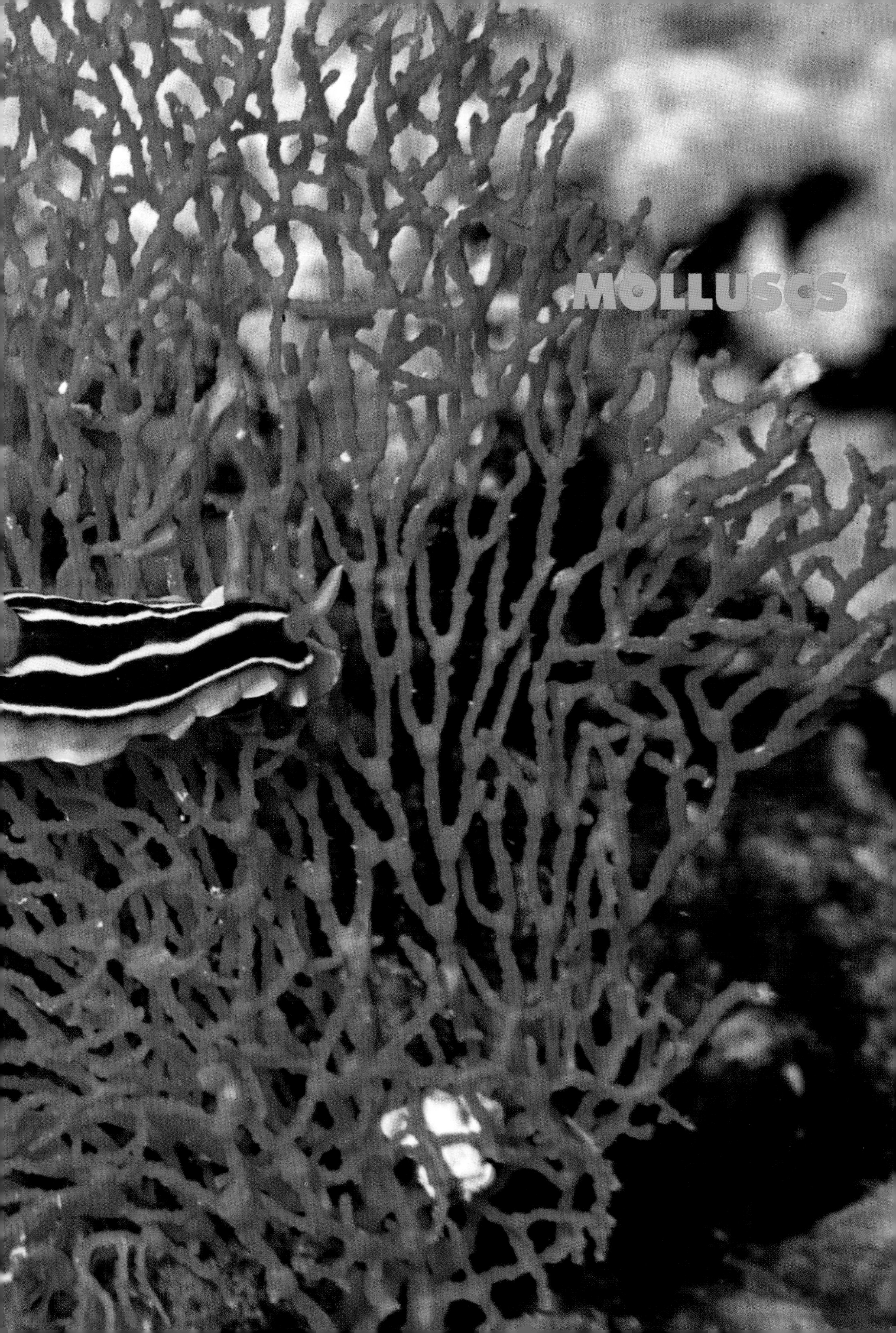

MOLLUSCS

MOLLUSCS

Sea shells have a fascinating appeal. They attract people of all ages and anyone who wanders over a coral reef wants to collect them. For the superabundance of molluscan life it contains, the South-West Pacific area, of which the Great Barrier Reef is an integral part, is probably unrivalled by any other region of similar extent. The warm shallow waters of this part of the world's oceans with their rich concentration of coral reefs have attracted the attention of shell collectors the world over. Shells which elsewhere are small, inconspicuous and drab may grow there to be giants of their species, displaying the most brilliant of colours.

Attractive as these shells are, they are only part of the complete living animal, and the most colourful and ornate sea shells are often rivalled by the beauty and delicacy of the animals they house. These animals are very soft without a backbone, and are called molluscs. Almost all are attached to their shells by strong muscles.

The study of shells is known as conchology and for the many people collecting colourful shells merely as a pleasant hobby this term would apply. On the other hand, there are the more serious-minded amateur collectors who also study the animals responsible for secreting the shells, and for them the term malacology is more correct.

Of the many divisions of Mollusca to be found on coral reefs the univalves, Gastropoda, are the most numerous. Although usually covered by a single external shell, some members carry their shell partly or wholly internally. A fleshy skin which lines the shell and covers the mollusc's body secretes the shell. Called a mantle, it is this remarkable organ which gives the infinite variety of pattern and design occurring in tropical marine shells. Molluscs move by means of a fleshy foot which in some univalves has a horny lid called an operculum. In most univalves the operculum is permanently attached to the foot and securely seals off the aperture of the shell when the animal withdraws. The mollusc's head is distinguishable and usually bears two or more feelers or tentacles. The eyes are small and are either located directly on the head, carried on tentacles or, as in the strombs, on separate stalks. It can be rather disquieting on examining one of these strombs to find a pair of curious eyes swivelling around to scrutinise one in return.

Most univalves are equipped with a ribbon-like tongue called a radula, which is a feeding organ furnished with numerous fine teeth. Its job is to break up plant and animal matter passing along its surface.

Bivalves form another group whose members are well represented on the reef. The animals in this group are protected by a pair of shelly valves usually of equal size, which are united towards the hinge line by a strong horny ligament. Movement of the valves is effected by contraction of powerful muscles which are attached to the inner face of each valve. Most bivalves possess two of these muscles but the oyster, for example, has only one. Some univalves are incapable of completely closing their shells and must remain slightly open, while others like clams and oysters are able to close themselves very tightly. Bivalves possess no radula but have a mouth which is located deep inside.

The wonderfully delicate, shell-less molluscs, the nudibranchs, are one of the more curious families of this division of animals. Although the shell is present in the larval stage it is soon discarded after hatching. A large selection of these beautiful and graceful animals can be seen in the waters of the Great Barrier Reef. Most species encountered are rather small and range from half an inch to three inches in length.

Perhaps the most colourful of these is *Chromodoris quadricolor*. The elongated, slug-like body of this species is electric blue in colour with broad bands of blackish purple, while the borders of the mantle and foot are edged with a brilliant orange-red. On the head are two tiny orange horn-like projections called rhinophores. These sensory organs are used to test the water and enable nudibranchs to sense each other's presence. A set of plume-like gills or branchiae can be seen on the dorsal surface towards the rear of the body. These are the chief means of respiration and it is from these naked gills that the name nudibranch is derived.

Much larger species occur and one of the best-known and most often illustrated is the splendid imperial dorid, *Hexabranchus imperialis*. This species reaches about ten inches in length and is commonly called the Spanish dancer or dancing lady because of its graceful swimming motion. The elaborate undulating movement which displays every beautiful fold and colour of its lovely mantle, makes this a favourite with the Great Barrier Reef visitor.

Some of the best-known tropical shells are the cowries (family Cypraeidae). Highly valued by people of the Indo-Pacific for ornamentation, one species, *Monetaria moneta*, was even used as a form of currency. With their highly enamelled polish, the most brilliant found in any shells, they have always been treasured by the casual reef fossicker and serious collector alike. Being typical tropical molluscs they reach their largest number of species and most brilliant colouring in the warm waters of the Great Barrier Reef.

Hunting for shells is always a favourite pastime on coral reefs; and cowries, because of their glossy shells, immediately attract the attention of all who encounter them. The animals which form these shells are often as vividly coloured and as attractive as the shells themselves. The mantle, which consists of two lobes, one extending up each side of the shell, is capable of completely concealing the shell from view. Where the two lobes meet at the top of the shell a line or break usually occurs in the patterning. With few exceptions the mantle lobes in cowries are ornamented with forked or pointed filaments or warty growths which the mollusc can expand or contract at will. The mantle lobes, which secrete the shell, extend to repair any scratch or blemish. Thus the extraordinarily beautiful gloss is maintained throughout the animal's life. In almost all other molluscs the mantle cannot extend this far so there is no chance of repair to a damaged shell.

Cowries are shy animals and once disturbed, immediately retract into their shell. Thus the attractive shell is fully exposed, often against a back ground of dead coral, looking almost too perfect to be real. In the daytime cowries usually remain concealed under rocks or hidden in crevices among the coral, whereas nightfall finds them wandering about in search of food.

The coral reefs produce many varieties of cowry which range in size from less than half an inch to four inches in length. Most of the larger ones live in the shallow waters of coral reefs, but some striking forms occur in the deep water of colder regions. Possibly the best known of all is the tiger cowry, *Cypraea tigris*, the largest cowry likely to be found by a visitor to the coral reef. This beautiful spotted shell is very common on the reefs of the Indo-Pacific region and favourite haunts are the shallow depressions in the living coral on the reef's edge. The sight of one of these molluscs on the coral growths with the shell fully exposed is quite unforgettable. If anyone is fortunate enough to find a specimen, a search of the surrounding coral could prove fruitful, as tiger cowries are usually found in pairs.

Another very abundant species not growing as large as *Cypraea tigris* is the milk-spotted cowry, *Cypraea vitellus*. Usually attaining a length of two and a half to three inches, the fawn-coloured shell has its upper surface covered with milk-white spots. Its habits differ from those of the tiger cowry in that it usually frequents the crevices and pockets beneath coral boulders, which have to be overturned to find the many smaller species of cowries. Many of these molluscs have adapted themselves to this particular environment, with mantles emulating the varied growths on the underside of the rocks.

Melward's cowry, *Nivigena melwardi*, is a one-inch long, much-prized species which has a pure white shell. The animal is scarlet and bears a remarkable resemblance to the scarlet sponge growths on which it lives.

Cowries are not the only molluscs likely to be disturbed when a coral boulder is overturned. Almost invariably an ass's ear shell *Haliotis asinina*, will be discovered. When disturbed, this ornate mollusc actively heads for the shelter of the nearest crevice and by means of its muscular foot is able to move quite rapidly. The smooth dark bluish green shell, attractively patterned with brown, is roughly oval in shape and is worn on the upper surface of the body, covering a portion only of the anterior half of the animal. When the mollusc is moving along with its beautifully green and cream mottled mantle fully expanded, the shell is almost completely hidden from view. Like all members of this family it is able to cling strongly to a flat surface by suction of the foot, and attempts to remove it are met with some resistance. Popularly called ear shells, due to their somewhat ear-like shape, they belong to the family Haliotidae, of which some larger members are important food sources in many countries where they are regarded as a delicacy.

Among the more abundant and certainly the most noticeable bivalves on the Great Barrier Reef are the clams. The largest of all living shells, giant tropical species reach over four feet in length and range throughout the Indo-Pacific including tropical Australian waters. There are at least four species on the Great Barrier Reef, three of them belonging to the genus *Tridacna* and one to the genus *Hippopus*, all of them are edible.

As they lie in the coral pools with the shell partly open they display along the inner border a wide expanse of mantle. This flesh or mantle ranges through all the colours of the spectrum. Myriads of tiny single-celled algae plants live in the protective tissues of the exposed mantle and clothe their host in exotic colours. The minute plants may not be merely decoration, for they possibly utilise the waste products produced by the clam and give off oxygen in return.

Although the flesh in a giant clam, *Tridacna gigas*, may weigh twenty-five pounds or more, and the pair of shells 500 pounds, this bivalve feeds only on the microscopic life in the sea. The large serrated shells of *Tridacna gigas* were once used by the inhabitants of the waterless islands of the coral reefs to catch and store rain-water. They were placed under pandanus trees, and long pieces of bark conveyed the water to the upturned shells. This clam is thought to live to a considerable age, even longer than the elephant. Impressive stories have been told of fishermen being trapped and held by it until they drowned, of divers being caught beneath the waves and dying within sight of the surface, but no authentic cases appear to have been recorded. There is not much chance of being caught in a clam located in the open. They are much too colourful and conspicuous to pass unnoticed. Older specimens, when covered by an abundance of marine growths, could perhaps be overlooked but the possibility of this occurring is remote.

Perhaps any danger from clams has been greatly exaggerated. If approached, there is a sudden jet of water, the mantle is withdrawn and the valves are rapidly locked shut. The animal is so sensitive that it partially withdraws into the shell when photographed underwater with flash. The sudden, intense light, which fish and other marine creatures ignore, in some way upsets a clam.

One of the largest univalves or gastropods inhabiting the waters of the Great Barrier Reef is the bailer or melon shell, *Melo amphora*. Although it may reach eighteen inches in length and is quite common in the sandy lagoons of the coral reefs, many visitors have never seen a living bailer. Although very active when hunting prey, as the tide falls these large univalves burrow beneath the sand by means of a huge fleshy foot. So rapidly do they burrow that in a very short time they disappear completely. Anyone walking these damp expanses of exposed sand may be quite unaware of the presence of a bailer. On the rising tide they again emerge from their sandy retreats and go ploughing across the sand-flats, pushing up a little bow wave of sand before them.

These animals are carnivores, living mainly on other molluscs, and are voracious feeders. As they move along they extend before them a curious trunk-like siphon. The main function of this is to draw a continual stream of clean water over the gills. The highly prized shell is smoothly rounded, with the large body whorl spined around its upper margin.

Externally, the shell on larger specimens is often weathered and sun-bleached. The interior of living shells is always a rich, glossy, apricot colour. Younger specimens are prettily ornamented with transverse bands of light brown and have a much more attractive shell. Another dweller of the sandy lagoon is the tun shell of which at least four species are found on the Great Barrier Reef. The most colourful and best-known of these is the partridge tun, *Cadus rufus*. This beautiful animal, marked in purplish brown and white, is very distinctive when seen fully extended. The shell, which grows to six inches long, is relatively light in texture and is protected by a light-coloured integument called a periostracum.

The cones are a group worthy of special attention. The family Conidae, belonging to the sub-order Toxoglossa, are characterised by the possession of venom apparatus. Of all the shell-bearing molluscs, cones are unique in that they are the only ones capable of inflicting a painful and sometimes fatal sting. This sting is delivered by the long tapered proboscis from which emerges the radular tooth. Cones should be handled with care and the animals should be picked up by the wide posterior end of the shell, preferably with gloves. Many casualties have been caused among humans by careless handling, but the animal usually withdraws into the shell when disturbed.

There are hundreds of species but their solid conical shape makes them easy to identify. Many have intricate, brilliantly marked patterning on the shells which is somewhat hidden in living specimens by a thin horny outer layer. Species which live in coral usually have the spire of the shell eroded or heavily covered with marine growths, but the sand dwellers have a much cleaner appearance. Being chiefly nocturnal in habit, they stay hidden under coral or buried in sand during the daytime, becoming active at night when they emerge to feed. Cones are carnivorous and feed by injecting venom into their prey which consists of worms, other gastropods and small fish.

Five Indo-Pacific species, all occurring on the Great Barrier Reef, all equipped with a well-developed venom apparatus and all definitely known to have inflicted stings on humans, are the marble cone, *Conus (Coronaxis) marmoreus*, cloth of gold cone, *Conus (Cylinder) textile*, tulip cone, *Conus (Tuliparia) tulipa*, court cone, *Conus (Regiconus) aulicus*, and the geographer cone, *Conus (Gastridium) geographus*. The latter was responsible for a fatality on the Great Barrier Reef in 1935, when a young man died a few hours after he was stung on the hand. The intensity of pain experienced as the result of a sting varies from one individual to another, and after the initial sting various symptoms occur. Numbness may begin at the wound site and spread, involving the whole body. Blurring of vision and paralysis can occur in severe cases, and the recovery period in less serious cases varies from a few hours to several weeks.

Each year the reefs and islands of the Great Barrier Reef are invaded by swarms of shell collectors. Some are once-in-a-life-time tourists who want attractive mementoes of their holiday, but there are some who plunder for profit. Whereas the tourists will take the few shells they happen to come across, the professionals, with their greater knowledge of the creatures' favourite haunts and more intensive reefing experience, will systematically strip a reef, taking every saleable shell. Not only do the molluscs become victims of human acquisitiveness, but sea-stars, crabs, sea-urchins, small fish, in fact anything that moves goes into the collecting bucket, and ends up, after the formalin treatment, as mummified remains in a collector's cabinet.

During the search for shells the coral boulders are overturned, exposing the multitude of animals to the harsh glare of sunlight. This may only disturb the inhabitants of the reef, without killing them; but when the coral boulders are overturned and left like that, either through ignorance or laziness, every creature dies or is forced to leave. Their world turned upside down, the delicate ones depending on coolness and shade are thrust into the harshness of the sun and wind. Those accustomed to sunlight are left in darkness. Areas of reef once throbbing with life have been converted into desert in this way. Whereas reefing, professional or amateur, may or may not bring a species close to extinction, destruction of the habitat most certainly will.

Above: Tiger Cowry, *Cypraea tigris*, with mantle lobes emerging and beginning to extend up the sides of the shell. The mantle secretes the shell and can repair any scratch or blemish

Left: Ass's Ear Shell, *Haliotis asinina*, crawling over the bottom of a colourful coral boulder. Incapable of retracting completely into its shell this mollusc is a tropical relative of the commercial Abalone. North-West Island, Capricorn Group

Above: Shell nearly hidden from view. Pointed filaments decorate the mantle

Above: With mantle fully extended, the Cowry glides along on its fleshy foot. Should it be disturbed it will immediately retract these lobes back into the shell

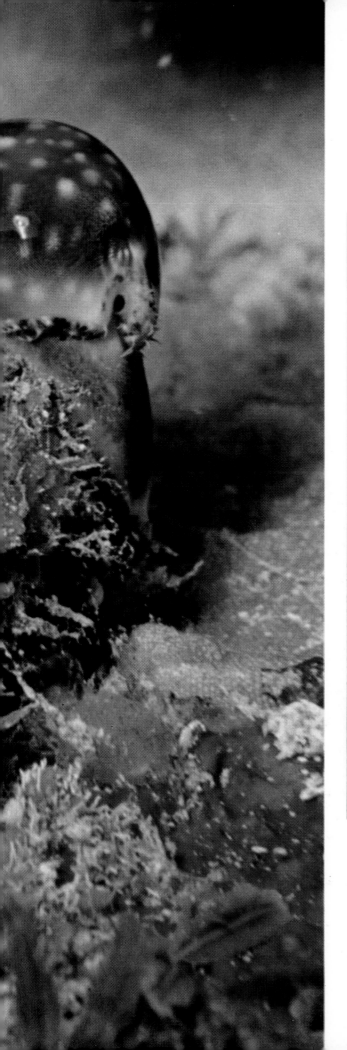

Above: One of the many delicate shell-less molluscs to be found on the Great Barrier Reef. From the group known as nudibranchs, this specimen, *Chromodoris quadricolor*, shows the flower-like gills exposed at rear which give the group their name. (This one was placed on the red Gorgonia for added colour and contrast.)

Left: Milk-Spotted Cowry, *Cypraea vitellus*, one of the most abundant of the Great Barrier Reef cowries

Left: Clam, *Tridacna maxima*, nestling amongst coral growths with its striking mantle exposed

Above: Gliding along on its enormous fleshy foot, this large Bailer, *Melo amphora*, extends its trunk-like siphon. Active when the tide is full, it buries itself beneath the sand when the tide ebbs

FOR PHOTOGRAPHERS

From time immemorial man has been fascinated by the sea. By peering into its depths his imagination has been stimulated by the relatively few marine creatures exposed to his gaze, and the contents of the abysms at which he could only guess. Now with the aid of modern diving equipment much of the sea and its infinite variety of inhabitants have become accessible to the many people who choose to penetrate its depths. The modern underwater photographer is in the unique position of being able not only to observe but also to record on film marine creatures in their colourful homes. It is a heartening sign that more and more of the younger skindivers of today are realising the futility of senselessly slaughtering marine life, and are replacing their spear-guns with underwater cameras. Competent skindivers thinking of taking up underwater photography have a clear advantage over other photographers since for any underwater activity, diving must be second nature.

I do not intend to go into detail about film, equipment and technique as that would require a book in itself. There are many excellent books available on the subject and anyone considering taking up this interesting field of photography can learn much about technique and equipment from them. However, it must be emphasised that time spent in the water perfecting technique by experimentation cannot be replaced by any amount of literature on the subject. I am merely setting down my personal choice of equipment, for the few who like to know what is used, and describing conditions likely to be encountered on a photographic trip to the Great Barrier Reef.

The cameras used for these photographs are two Rolleiflex 3.5F fitted into the Rolleimarin underwater casings Nos. 3 and 4. Film used is the 2¼ x 2¼ inch size. This will probably bring cries of anguish from owners of 35mm. cameras and I realise that modern precision lenses and photographic emulsions have largely eliminated the advantages the larger-size negatives used to have. However, when operating underwater I believe every possible advantage, however slight, is a necessity. I have the Rolleimarin No. 3 fitted with a close-up lens which enables me to photograph as close to the subject as eight inches. The other underwater camera, No. 4, has interchangeable lenses and, with its range of sixteen inches to infinity, gives complete coverage.

Both cameras are hung beneath the boat on nylon rope fitted with quick-release clips, and can be used when required. The two cameras between them give twenty-four shots, and I consider only twelve shots to a roll of film to be a minor disadvantage of the Rolleimarin underwater. Although almost all literature on under-water photography recommends the use of a wide-angle lens, for the type of work I do the 75mm. lens of the Rolleiflex is ideal. Naturally, there have been times when I have felt the need for a wide-angle lens, and for anyone planning to photograph divers and their various activities this type of lens would be a necessity.

I have found that the most suitable area of the Great Barrier Reef for underwater photography is around the Capricorn Group of islands and adjacent reefs. Most of the photographs in this book were taken in this area.

The northern part of the reef has a wider variety of marine life but the proximity of mainland rivers pouring large quantities of fine silt into the sea, which remains in suspension affecting visibility, spoils this area to some extent for underwater photography. I prefer the winter months from about June to September, as the seas are more often calmer and clearer during this period. Activity underwater is a little quieter as there are not so many sharks about and the turtles do not usually begin to arrive until September, but the main reef-dwellers and marine growths are there in abundance and present unlimited subjects for the camera. From mid-October onwards, strong winds begin to blow, whipping up heavy seas with resultant dirty water. It can be very frustrating to have beautiful hot sunny days with clear skies, yet incessant winds and heavy seas for weeks at a time.

The time of day does not seem to make much difference to water clarity but the high and low of the tide, when the water is still before the run begins, often give good results. Many people expect the waters of the Great Barrier Reef to be always crystal clear, and stories of being able to read newspaper headlines on the bottom through forty feet of water are sometimes true. But even in clear waters of the Capricorn Group there is a great difference between looking straight down from the deck of a boat, and entering the water and then looking along. I have watched a spider shell, *Lambis lambis*, moving over the coral rubble sixty feet beneath the boat off Fitzroy Lagoon, the water apparently crystal clear. However, on diving in I was surprised to find masses of sizeable sediment floating along in the current. The water had a definite smoky haze, which limited horizontal visiblity, and photography in these conditions would not have resulted in successful pictures.

The clarity of the water varies from day to day and from hour to hour. One can be busily working in clear water when cloudy conditions come rolling in like a fog, making photography impossible within ten minutes. Sediment is of course present in sea water, no matter how clear, so the underwater photographer has to live with it and learn to overcome it in various ways. If using flash, sediment can be a problem, as any floating near the lens reflects too much light and shows up on the film as harsh, blurry spots. This can be eliminated to some extent by mounting the flash reflector on an extension which holds it out to the side of the casing. Most underwater cameras on the market today are fitted out in this way. A means of operating when the water is too murky for average distance photography is to fit a close-up lens and get in really close.

The less water there is between the lens and the subject, the less light-diffusing sediment there is also.

For serious work a boat is necessary, as it is no joke to heave breathing apparatus, cameras and other equipment over a coral reef. I use a fourteen-foot aluminium Quintrex fitted with a 33 h.p. Evinrude motor, and find this combination ideal. If first-class results are required, breathing equipment is necessary when recording marine life and its activities. In recent years I have been using hookah breathing apparatus in preference to the aqualung because it eliminates the filling and handling of heavy air cylinders. There is the additional safety factor of being attached to the boat at all times—a very important consideration when working among coral reefs with swirling currents present which can often carry one away from the boat. Several plastic bottles with lengths of wire cables are used to mark areas which have to be revisited, for fish and other marine creatures do not always perform or appear when the photographer wishes. Wire cable is necessary as rope quickly frays on the coral.

On my last visit to the Reef I stayed for some months and during this time many of the markers began to disappear. As there had been no heavy seas the cause remained a mystery until I discovered the culprits were parrot fish. After several weeks, that part of the plastic float which was beneath the surface became heavily coated with weed. The parrot fish, while feeding on this, were crushing the bottom of the markers, thus allowing water to enter and leaving them afloat just beneath the surface.

The field of underwater photography has enormous potential as an aid to the study of marine biology, providing the scientific worker with pictorial information about marine life. The photographer should try to record his subject in its actual habitat. If photographs of specimens in other surroundings, such as aquariums, are to be published, their setting must be stated, otherwise the scientist may be misled regarding the animal's habitat. In recording such activities as breeding or egg-laying, a photograph is of more value if it is dated and accompanied by notes on locality and depth. Nothing can be quite as exasperating to a marine biologist as to be confronted with a photograph of some unknown species or rare activity and, on inquiring where and when it was taken, to find that the photographer made no notes at the time and has since forgotten.

INDEX